MANAGER'S GUIDE TO CONTINGENCY PLANNING FOR DISASTERS

5·17·2022

MANAGER'S GUIDE TO CONTINGENCY PLANNING FOR DISASTERS

Protecting Vital Facilities and Critical Operations

SECOND EDITION

KENNETH N. MYERS

JOHN WILEY & SONS, INC.

New York • Chichester • Weinheim • Brisbane • Singapore • Toronto

Library of Congress Cataloging-in-Publication Data:

ISBN 0-471-35838-X

Printed in the United States of America.

10   9   8   7   6   5   4   3

To Marcia

ABOUT THE AUTHOR

Kenneth N. Myers is an internationally recognized contingency planning specialist. Since 1972, he has been president of K. N. Myers & Associates, Inc., in Annapolis, Maryland, and has prepared disaster contingency plans for leading organizations throughout the United States, Europe, Mexico, and Puerto Rico. Myers uses the copyrighted plan development process contained in this book to complete prototype contingency plans in 30 days. He has appeared on the Financial Management Network's *Business Tonight* and is featured in continuing education segments for the Financial Management Network. Mr. Myers developed curricula for disaster recovery planning seminars for the Battelle Institute and the American Management Association and was called to New York to consult with the largest tenant in the World Trade Center II following its bombing. He is also the author of *Total Contingency Planning for Disasters: Managing Risk . . . Minimizing Loss . . . Ensuring Business Continuity.*

CONTENTS

CONTENTS

CONTENTS

CONTENTS

CONTENTS

PREFACE

Manager's Guide to Contingency Planning for Disasters describes why "what if" business continuity strategies are sufficient given the low probability of a disaster; and that developing detailed scenarios and procedures are a waste of time and money.

Developing a contingency plan is not crossing every "t" and dotting every "i" or preparing detailed "weigh it by the pound" reports that are the hallmark of most consulting firms. It does not require an involved "business impact analysis" to gain consensus on the relative criticality of different business functions. *Manager's Guide* explains that what is "critical" under normal operating conditions when all systems are operational and what is "critical" at the time a disaster happens differ *depending on what options are available* following a disaster to maintain business continuity.

Developing a contingency plan is not preparing individual scenarios and responses for different types of disasters, nor is it itemizing different responses based on the expected duration of the interruption. *Manager's Guide* recommends that only a "worst-case" scenario be used in developing "what if" business continuity strategies, with the understanding that less serious conditions could reasonably be expected to be handled within this framework.

Developing a contingency plan is not spending thousands of dollars for a plan development process that lasts several months and takes valuable time from line managers. *Manager's Guide* suggests an approach anchored in a practical corporate contingency plan policy and strategy, and emphasizes *survival* rather than "business as usual" following a disaster.

1

INTRODUCTION

MANAGEMENT'S RESPONSIBILITY

If economics is the "dismal science," then contingency planning must be "abysmal science." No one likes to look into the abyss. But given the critical dependence of businesses on technology, facilities, and specialized processes, contingency planning for disasters is a rising priority on the agenda of senior management.

Who should do the planning? Who can ensure that the plan is actually workable? The most serious mistake is to have a plan that exists only on paper, without the understanding or support of line managers who would have to use it to stabilize operations following a disaster. The most costly mistake is to have a plan aimed at keeping computers running instead of keeping the *business* running. The most common mistake is a plan that focuses on computer disasters but ignores potential physical disasters that can render vital buildings inaccessible or critical operations inoperable.

HOW MUCH MARKET SHARE WILL IT COST YOU?

A disaster could happen to you, for whatever reason—fire, explosion, sabotage by a disgruntled employee or former employee:

- A vital office building is severely damaged or destroyed, and restoring computer operations will take longer than hoped for. Where will administrative personnel be relocated? What is the minimum number of personnel (you certainly do not need 100 percent of normal

1

staff) for which space is required during a "stabilization period"—how many could temporarily work from home? What backup strategy is there for entering and handling customer orders? How is everyone going to be paid on Friday? The answer is to develop and document flexible *business continuity strategies* that can be used to stabilize operations until operations return to normal.

• A critical production operation or distribution facility is severely damaged. What alternatives exist to continue production? What locations are most viable? How will you track inventory and production? How will you operate distribution centers? Perhaps most importantly, in a crisis of this magnitude, can you continue to service customers and maintain market share? The answer is to develop and document business continuity strategies to ensure continuity in production and distribution until operations return to normal.

PROTECT AGAINST WHAT?

For many years, the only concern for contingency planning seemed to be the temporary loss of data processing capability because that was the area first targeted by outside auditors. In fact, the real threat to business continuity is in the loss of vital buildings or critical production or distribution operations resulting from natural causes, sabotage, or environmental conditions. Outside auditors and internal auditors are pressing management to extend their contingency plans for computers to include protection against the temporary loss of access to buildings. The problem is that the mindset, policy and strategy, and approach that were successful in addressing contingency planning for data processing are not appropriate for facility contingency planning.

Facility contingency planning is an exercise in long-range strategic planning and, as such, should be conducted by a "neutral" facilitator, not someone in a line organization or information systems staff. The detailed specifications and procedures required to back up and restore computer data are not needed to ensure business continuity in operating departments. It is difficult to keep information systems personnel from unconsciously gravitating to more and more detail because that is the way computer systems are designed. Information systems should be responsible for identifying data processing restoration strategy; a staff planner or outside facilitator should be responsible for developing facility contingency plans.

Mindset is also different between protecting computer processing and protecting against loss of facilities. If computer equipment is damaged or destroyed, restoring operations requires precise, systematic, tightly controlled and disciplined detailed procedures. The solutions are technical and highly structured; there are few options. This is not true for administrative departments or manufacturing operations or distribution activities. In administrative departments and production operations, there can be several different options that might be used to ensure business continuity, depending on the nature of the physical disaster, the amount of damage, and the prognosis for reentering the building. Implementation of specific actions should be left to the judgment of department managers to decide at the time a disaster actually occurs.

In addition, senior management intuitively understands that a detailed plan covering multiple combinations of types of disaster just does not make sense. They understand that highly skilled individuals head up key departments and that those individuals do not need detailed instructions on *how* to carry out their responsibilities, they only need to agree on strategies.

CONTINGENCY PLANNING REQUIRES SPECIALIZATION

In determining who might develop a plan, be leery of turning the assignment over to a consulting firm that offers a broad range of services. There can be several problems. Consulting firms shuffle staff between assignments, many times without much hands-on experience in facility contingency planning; this can result in confusion, false starts, time delays, and excessive costs. They usually charge per diem fees, which are counterproductive, tie up key personnel in lengthy meetings, encourage unnecessarily lengthy "weigh it by the pound" reports, and produce "politically correct" reports, all of which drive up contingency planning costs unnecessarily. Most consulting firms are trained in a problem-solving process that emphasizes detail, detail, and more detail; exactly the opposite of "what if" strategies that are the key to cost-effective contingency planning.

INCREASED TECHNOLOGY DEPENDENCY

Today's children are more comfortable with automation and computer technology than their parents are. Is it any wonder that a "generation gap" is a constant in dealing with computers? In but a short time, data processing has advanced from electronic accounting machines, for which each individual step of logic had to be programmed by connecting a wire from one "hub" to another, to technology enabling computers to speak and understand verbal expressions.

In the business world, computer technology has skyrocketed from tabulating historical accounting transactions to the real-time assimilation of complex analog and digital data and the formulation and execution of process control procedures with unheralded quality assurance. Computers have the capability to consistently assimilate variable data, to develop solutions, and to apply that capability to a multitude of business problems.

If we are not careful, this will lead us to a conclusion that *all* computer systems are indispensable, even for short periods of time. Nothing could be further from the truth. Although computerized "process control" systems may be indispensable in specific production environments, most management information systems are not.

For instance, most people assume that airlines are so dependent on computer systems, particularly passenger reservation systems, that they have already arranged for off-site redundant processing capability in the event of a disaster. Most major airlines do not have off-site redundant computer processing capability, and their most critical system is not passenger reservations, but *airplane maintenance.*

Redundant off-site processing capability has been rejected because of its cost. They are also confident that computer processing capability will be restored before it causes significant *long-term* loss of market share.

Why are businesses convinced that computerized management information systems are indispensable, even for short periods of time? For most organizations, computer dependency during a disaster recovery period is a myth precipitated by these factors:

• Absence of a focused awareness and education program.
• Failure to explore alternatives.

4

An educational process and the exploration of viable alternatives with the right people are the key to cost-effective contingency planning.

Foreign Corrupt Practices Act

The Foreign Corrupt Practices Act, probably more than anything else, increased awareness of the lack of contingency planning in corporate America.

The Foreign Corrupt Practices Act points out that computerized management information systems contribute to the decision-making process and management's control of operations, and as such, represent the lifeline of an organization. It further indicates that management planning related to the continued availability of these decision-making systems has, for directors and high-level officers, an impact on the standards of care. Moreover, these standards would be applied in determining potential liability if, for example, lack of a contingency plan resulted in avoidable business losses. Therefore, management can be held liable for inadequate contingency plans. For highlights of the Foreign Corrupt Practices Act, see Exhibit 1.1.

Exhibit 1.1 Highlights of Foreign Corrupt Practices Acts

- Because of the large investment in computer software development, the resultant programs and related data bases are considered as much an asset as buildings and equipment.

- Just as insurance policies are used to protect physical assets, reasonable steps should be taken to prevent information processing capability disasters.

- Because computerized information processing is the lifeblood of many businesses, the protection of computer processing capability is no longer the sole responsibility of the data processing manager but extends to the board of directors.

- If businesses elect not to develop a loss prevention and business continuity plan, then they should have a well-documented analysis that justifies their position in the event of legal action by stockholders.

- Directors and management can be held personally and criminally liable for damages if they knowingly neglect this exposure.

Interpretation Problem

Unfortunately, the most prestigious auditing firms made a mistake in communicating their interpretation of the Foreign Corrupt Practices Act to clients. The mistake was the context in which contingency planning was addressed in annual management letters. Management letters are traditionally written at the conclusion of an audit to, among other things, highlight internal control weaknesses discovered as a result of their "test of transactions," and recommend corrective action to address those weaknesses.

In management letters, auditors criticized clients for *"lack of a computer disaster recovery plan."* This was wrong! What should have been criticized was "lack of a business continuity plan in the event of an interruption in data processing capability." Putting emphasis on computer technology rather than on business continuity was the error. Exhibit 1.2 illustrates the impact of the Foreign Corrupt Practices Act on business.

The results of that mistake were compounded by senior management's assigning responsibility to data processing for what should have been a business continuity plan. The problem is that business continuity planning is a type of long-range strategic planning, and results are optimized when orchestrated by a skilled, neutral facilitator. Most data processing

Exhibit 1.2   Impact of Foreign Corrupt Practices Act

- Computer programs and computerized data are assets.

- Auditors criticized clients for lack of a *computer disaster* recovery plan. (Instead, they should have criticized the lack of a *business continuity plan.*)

- Businesses wrongly assumed that data processing should prepare the plan. (Business continuity planning is a type of long-range strategic planning and should not be delegated to the data processing department.)

- As a result, many plans focused on restoring computer operations instead of ensuring business continuity during a brief disaster recovery period.

- Unnecessary and costly backup computer hot-site agreements were negotiated as a result of misdirected plan development strategy and lack of a plan development methodology that emphasized the importance of cost-effective solutions.

---

personnel are neither skilled in facilitating a long-range planning process nor independent from the solution.

CORPORATE ISSUE

Because disaster recovery and business continuity planning involves long-range planning considerations, it must support the business plan. There are generally three areas of exposure to be addressed:

1. Loss of communications
2. Loss of computer processing capability
3. Loss of access to facilities

Although administrative responsibility for functional areas may be controlled by individual departments, contingency planning must be centrally coordinated. Interdepartmental interfaces, dependency of one system on others, and the need to reduce duplicate planning point to the need for a well-coordinated corporatewide contingency planning process.

DISASTER LIFE CYCLE

In deciding what should be included in a facility contingency plan, it is helpful to understand the different phases of a disaster. Although a complete disaster life cycle consists of four time periods (see Exhibit 1.3), only three deliverables should be included in a contingency plan:

1. Risk management program
2. Emergency response plan
3. Business continuity strategies

Long-range restoration strategy will depend on the specific nature of the disaster that occurred, damage assessment, and prognosis for re-entering the building. You might be back in the building in four weeks or you might need to construct a whole new facility. So until a specific disaster happens, it does not make much sense to try and anticipate where,

Exhibit 1.3   Disaster Life Cycle

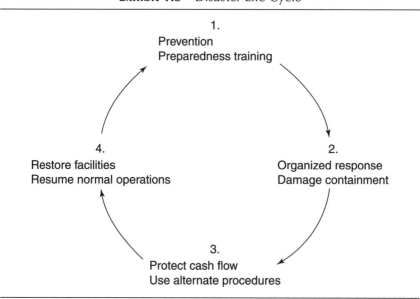

when, or how you will resume normal operations. That will be decided later by senior management, and a statement to that effect should be part of the corporate contingency planning policy and strategy.

Risk Management Program

Because most organizations will never experience a serious facility disaster, a risk management program is the only part of a plan that will ever be used; there will never be an opportunity to actually exercise an emergency response plan nor will there be a need to call business continuity strategies into service. However, a sound risk management program is indeed important because it consists of ongoing activities that help prevent the likelihood of a disaster, such as sound physical security measures, and minimizes impact of a disaster, such as storing duplicate computer records off-site so that they can be recovered. Risk management programs should be institutionalized, that is, key responsibilities should be integrated into job descriptions and included in annual performance evaluations. A risk management program consists of all activities and responsibilities, the purpose of which is to reduce the likelihood of a disaster either to a building or to the business functions located in that building.

A risk management program is *procedural* in format because its purpose is to document ongoing responsibilities.

Emergency Response Plan

An emergency response plan is only called into action at the time a physical disaster occurs and covers the first 24 to 48 hours following a disaster. For purposes of this book, it includes primarily issues that demand immediate attention and/or are prerequisites to maintaining business continuity; however, it does not include strategies for maintaining business continuity during a *stabilization period* as they appear in the Business Continuity Strategies section.

The most essential issues to be included in an emergency response plan are:

- Notification to employees and customers
- Damage assessment
- Rerouting incoming phone calls and/or messaging
- Initiating restoring computer processing capability
- Physical security
- Relocating personnel

Detailed commentary about treating injuries, health-care procedures, or other services normally provided by government or municipal agencies, departments, or institutions, are not recommended for inclusion in an emergency response plan. It should be assumed that these agencies, departments, and institutions will perform as expected, although not as quickly in a regional disaster.

An emergency response plan has a *checklist* format because it consists of issues that should not be overlooked in the excitement and trauma immediately following a physical disaster.

Business Continuity Strategies

Business continuity strategies are pivotal "what if" strategies for maintaining business continuity following a disaster and are developed through highly structured discussions with department line managers and key supervisors. If they are not developed with the right mindset and expectations; are not facilitated by an individual experienced in synergistic problem solving, and do not focus exclusively on basic business functions (not computer systems), they will be part of the problem instead of part of the solution. In a worst-case scenario, one in which a building is assumed inaccessible for as long as six weeks and computer processing may not be restored for up to 10 working days, two strategies need to be addressed:

1. What actions will be taken to perform tasks, such as processing customer orders and maintaining inventory status, until computer processing capability is restored?
2. What actions will be taken to stabilize operations, such as servicing customers and maintaining market share until operations return to normal?

Developing practical business continuity strategies with line managers is where many otherwise sound plans have foundered. It involves the sensitive encounter of first-line managers and supervisors. Discomfort, insecurity, and even fear are mixed in with their logical and professional responses. If these factors are not acutely understood and carefully dealt with, they can quickly harden into resistance or evasion.

Specialists facilitating development of these "what if" strategies must respect the department managers as well as the delicate structure of an organization's policy. Only then will department managers perceive that their opinions count. It is the one part of developing a contingency plan that it is worth the expense of using a specialist skilled in this highly sensitive process because it involves a different mindset and a unique problem-solving technique.

Business continuity strategies are documented as *guidelines* because they only represent options. Department managers will determine precisely how they will proceed based on the nature of a specific incident combined with an assessment of damage.

DISCRETIONARY EXPENSE

When the economic climate is favorable, contingency planning is last on the list of things to do; when profits are down, contingency planning is the first item to be cut from the budget. Like elective surgery, contingency planning is a discretionary expense. This means that the more

Exhibit 1.4   Plan Building Blocks

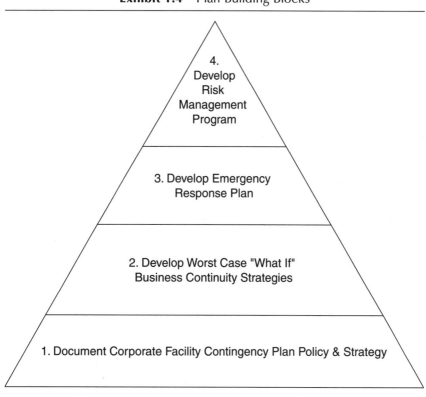

4.
Develop
Risk
Management
Program

3. Develop Emergency
Response Plan

2. Develop Worst Case "What If"
Business Continuity Strategies

1. Document Corporate Facility Contingency Plan Policy & Strategy

costly a contingency planning project is, the more likely it is that it will be repeatedly deferred.

Given that contingency planning is a discretionary cost-sensitive issue, there are two areas on which to focus in such planning:

1. Keep costs at a minimum by using a plan development methodology designed to yield cost-effective solutions.
2. Minimize testing requirements by encouraging "plain vanilla" business continuity solutions that, because of their simplicity, require less exotic testing procedures.

For a representation of plan building blocks, see Exhibit 1.4.

2

DEFINING THE PROBLEM

BUSINESS CONTINUITY CONCERNS

Common areas of exposure to a disaster for a business include the following:

- Telephone communications
- Computer processing
- Vital facilities
- Critical operations

Telephone Communications

Telephones are often taken for granted; they are seldom out of service except for brief periods, such as immediately following a storm. Older electromechanical telephone switching equipment was extremely reliable. However, consumer demand for more sophisticated service has resulted in a conversion from electromechanical to software-controlled switching systems. The advantage of such systems is that they are easily modified to provide more sophisticated options to customers. The downside is increased vulnerability to periodic interruptions in telephone service owing to software malfunction. Every time computer software is changed, the risk of error increases—error that may lie dormant for months until the weakness is exposed. Moreover, it is unrealistic to expect all software changes to be sufficiently tested to preclude failure. Many of the features are new, and models for testing are, by definition, incomplete. Therefore, it is appropriate to prepare a contingency plan that will provide minimum voice communication capability during a stabilization period.

Computer Processing

Financial service organizations cannot operate for more than a day or two without computer processing, as they need this capability to service transactions.

Yet for many other organizations, this is not the case. Although many businesses are dependent on computers for day-to-day operations, it is incorrect to assume that they could not operate without this support during a relatively brief disaster recovery period that might last a week or two. The difficult part is focusing on the right issue—keeping the business running, rather than keeping the computer running.

Operating without Computer Processing Capability. Manufacturers can be exposed to several problems if computer processing is inoperable. However, careful analysis usually concludes that although inefficient, product can still be manufactured and shipped without normal computer processing support. Alternate business continuity strategies and prerequisites for manufacturing without normal computer support need to be negotiated with functional managers. Prerequisites, such as starting points, need to be included in the risk management program section of a business contingency plan to ensure that they will be available when needed. For example, it is not that storeroom inventories cannot be updated without an on-line computer, the problem is lack of a "starting point," or in other words, a record of what the inventory file looked like when the computer outage occurred. So if a risk management program includes daily responsibility to store offsite a duplicate copy of the storeroom inventory file, immediately following a computer disaster the file could be printed at another location and delivered to manufacturing as a snapshot of inventory locations and availability. Receipts and disbursements could easily be retained with a simple personal computer (PC) spreadsheet until normal computer processing is restored. See Exhibit 2.1 for vital manufacturing support functions.

Headquarter operations can also be exposed to problems if computer processing is suddenly inoperable. However, careful analysis again usually concludes that although inefficient, business can still continue and

Exhibit 2.1   Vital Manufacturing Support Functions

- Take orders
- Schedule production
- Order material
- Receive and store material
- Control inventory
- Pick items
- Manufacture
- Ship
- Invoice

customers can still be serviced without normal computer processing support. It helps to look at administrative business functions and what alternatives are available to get the job done without computer processing.

Insurance providers are concerned about issues such as new business underwriting; determining "in force" for claims adjudication; beneficiary information; and exposure for coverage that would have been canceled under normal circumstances. In each of these instances, there are alternative strategies that, although inefficient and cumbersome, can be used to ensure business continuity until computer processing is restored.

Distributors need strategies for taking and processing orders that are normally entered into computer data bases, identifying kitting requirements, producing picking documents, inventory management, producing shipping documentation, and handling returns. The question to be asked is not "what problems would you have?"; it is "if confronted with this situation, what would you do to maintain market share and service customers until normal operations resume?"

Associations and agencies are concerned about membership services, legislation and public policy, publications, research, education and training, call centers, and government regulations. In most instances, the overriding consideration is to seek solutions for operating temporarily without normal computer processing capability that will not require continual funding, such as a computer hot-site agreement, but would ensure continuity in servicing members, volunteers, and staff during a stabilization period.

Alternate business continuity strategies for meeting administrative responsibilities without normal computer support need to be negotiated with department managers. The window of *expected* outage must be determined. For the most part, information systems managers consistently agree that they could restore computer processing capability within 10 working days (14 calendar days). So the question to be asked of department managers is not "how long can you do without . . ." or "what do you need . . ."; managers tend to understate and pad the first question, and in response to the second question will tend to ask for more than they need. Both questions beg answers and initiate thought processes that are not conducive to cost-effective contingency planning and invite discussions and deliberations that require further documentation and maintenance expense. The only question to ask line managers in relation to doing without normal computer processing is "what alternate strategies could be used to continue functioning for approximately 10 days without computer processing capability?" When *that* question is asked, 99% of the responses are positive, that is, department managers are willing to accept operating at less than 100% efficiency and admit what could be done to meet the challenge of temporarily working without computer processing.

The simple psychology and willingness of contingency planners to "stick their necks out" and insist on establishing a reasonable limit to an expected computer outage will, in turn, have the positive effect of persuading line managers to admit how they could survive. Establishing this "window" up front is the key to a collaborative solution. But also remember that in establishing the window, information systems managers must also accept some risk and not pad their expected recovery capability. The question is not "when are they absolutely positive beyond any reasonable doubt that computer processing will be restored?"; rather, it is "given emergency conditions, working 24 hours a day, seven days a week, with adequate resources, when is it likely that computer processing could be restored?" On-line connectivity can wait because there are other solutions available, but being able to process data is the important requirement. See Exhibit 2.2 for a list of typical administrative business functions.

Y2K Fall-Back Plan. Y2K computer problems could be caused by a myriad of conditions. Power grids could fail due to unanticipated drops

Exhibit 2.2   Typical Administrative Business Functions

- Inventory management
- Order processing
- Scheduling
- Billing
- Receivables
- Payables
- General accounting
- Payroll
- Human resources
- Data processing

---

in demand (as users of questionable systems delay initializing opera-tions, either because corrective work has not been completed or because of other concerns) which are so severe that the power companies must bring down and reconfigure power systems grids nationally. Failure of satellite communications, HVAC (heating, ventilation, air conditioning, and cooling) systems, automated processing equipment, and computer hardware or software are all possible. The broad and diversified nature of this potential problem is such that testing cannot ensure that some sys-tems might not fail.

One-time potential problem issues such as Y2K have two dimensions. The first is to identify steps that need to be taken to reduce the likelihood of computer-dependent operations from being interrupted, and monitor-ing compliance with those programs, within reason. Without careful over-sight by informed senior management, this approach can wind up being a boondoggle for consulting firms—fear tactics, an inordinate amount of "analysis" and "weigh it by the pound" reports, endless meetings, and a large consulting bill.

Most important, however, is to develop a Y2K fall-back plan that will ensure business continuity even if computer-dependent operations are temporarily inoperable. Experience and common sense suggest that a Y2K fall-back plan is the safety net that needs to be in place, and organ-izations that already have a business continuity plan for loss of computer processing already have one. It just needs to be dusted off and modified slightly, and it can easily be used as a Y2K fall-back plan. Conversely, if an organization does not already have a disaster recovery and business continuity plan for loss of computer processing, now is the time to prepare one because it will solve both problems. Chances are that if there are failures, they will be isolated and will be corrected in a matter of days, if not hours. See Exhibit 2.3 for a Y2K fall-back plan development strategy.

Vital Facilities

The loss of buildings resulting from fire and other accidents is not a new threat. Nor are there any miraculous solutions. Insurance is still the most cost-effective answer. Business failure following a disaster is normally caused by a loss of assets, such as a manufacturing facility, distribution center, or office building, or an inability to support vital business functions following a disruption in normal processing capability. An inability to support vital business functions immediately following a publicized disaster can be devastating when this information is in the hands of competitors. If orders are "lost," customer service communications lines are inoperable, or inventory availability records become unreliable, even if only for a few days, it can result in a significant loss of market

---

Exhibit 2.3 Y2K Fall-Back Plan Development Strategy

- Identify computer-dependent vendors and services.
- Identify business functions dependent on computer processing.
- Fund and monitor a prevention program.
- Obtain senior management's approval of a corporate policy and strategy for a Y2K fall-back plan.
- Develop "what if" business continuity strategies for all potentially affected business functions to protect market share and support customer service, even if normal computing capability is not available for a few days.
- Add a risk management program.
- Add an emergency response plan.

---

share, particularly with the 20 percent of a company's customers that make up 80 percent of its revenue. Most organizations have not adequately addressed the issue of how to keep the business running if a plant or office building was inaccessible for several days. In other words, the concern is not what to do if assets are destroyed, but how to continue to operate a business if primary work locations are temporarily inaccessible or unusable.

Operating without Access to Vital Facilities or Critical Operations, or "Forget the Computer, How Will We Ship Product?" In many production and manufacturing facilities, losing normal computer processing capability would have a serious impact on efficiency, order processing, scheduling, and tracking orders, but it would not destroy the ability to somehow manually shepherd product through the manufacturing and shipping process. Efficiency would suffer; record keeping would become a nightmare, excess inventory would have to be ordered (and worked off later) to avoid stock-outs, and production rates would drop, but product would get out the door.

Losing access to an entire production facility or one critical operation could, in many instances, bring manufacturing to a halt. Without alternate solutions to ship product until operations return to normal, business failure could result. It is this possibility and its impact on cash flow that demands that companies have contingency plans for loss of normal computer processing capability and "what if" strategies for a temporary loss of access to production facilities.

Raw material and component parts might be sent to alternate manufacturing sources; components might be purchased instead of manufactured; excess regional production capacities might be temporarily leased; "second-choice" production alternatives might be approved; inspection and quality control procedures might be changed; and some items might be shipped direct. The important issue is for manufacturing managers to take the time to "think through" which alternatives are most likely to work and which are most cost effective. It is important that these alternate production methods or "what if" strategies be documented in writing so that: (1) their workability can be validated annually; (2) any prerequisites, such as maintaining daily backup copies of inventory status reports or files offsite to support alternate manufacturing methods, can be identified and inserted into a risk management program; and (3) crisis management activities, such as using the most recent stock status reports as a basis for insurance claims, are added to the emergency response plan.

Only a Computer Recovery Plan

Which comes first, the chicken or the egg? Which comes first in contingency planning? Recovering lost technology or keeping the business running? *The business continuity plan should come first.* In fact, data processing plans to recover technology that are developed before business continuity strategies are explored, normally result in an excessive amount of resources committed to redundant computer processing capability. Auditors are becoming increasingly critical of the lack of business continuity plans and are beginning to emphasize this area more than the loss of processing technology. After all, what good is a restored computer if users are unable to keep the business running immediately following a disaster? If you are just getting started in contingency planning, you should address the business continuity issue *before* you worry about redundant computer processing capability.

Present Plan May Not Work

Less than 25 percent of business organizations have a workable disaster recovery plan. Some plans look good on paper—but would not work if they had to be implemented. Plans that are not viable usually have three things in common:

1. The focus is on keeping the computer running rather than on keeping the business running.
2. No one has taken the time to identify alternate procedures to support functions that *normally* rely on computer technology, but could actually survive a stabilization period using alternate methods.
3. The plan contains unnecessary detail and professes to cope with problems that are typically nonexistent.

Exhibit 2.4 lists common reasons that many disaster recovery plans will not work.

Exhibit 2.4 Common Disaster Recovery Plan Problems

- Focus on recovering computer technology at costly hot sites, rather than on sustaining business continuity until temporary computer processing capability can be restored locally.

- Lack of an awareness and education program that positions functional managers so that they understand the importance of their input and are willing to participate in plan development.

- Alternate procedures not explored that could sustain vital business functions (that normally are dependent on centralized computer processing) until computer processing capability is restored.

- Excessively detailed procedures developed when guidelines were all that were needed.

CHARACTERISTICS OF A SOUND PLAN

A contingency plan should be reviewed annually to ensure compatibility with business practices and to integrate lessons learned from new disasters and test results into more cost-effective solutions. Many times, it is helpful to have someone other than the individual who developed the plan to conduct such a review. It is difficult to be objective when reviewing your own work.

A *corporate contingency planning policy and strategy* approved by senior management is a requirement. This document should emphasize that (1) providing 100 percent redundancy for all types of physical disasters is simply not practical; (2) documenting detailed alternate procedures for an infinite number of combinations of possible disasters is also not realistic and would create a "monster" to maintain; and (3) departmental managers are the architects of "what if" business continuity strategies that will serve as guidelines to ensure business continuity following a disaster.

Assumptions under which a plan is developed should be stated to clarify expectations and avoid excessive documentation. The following list is an example of assumptions:

21

- Qualified personnel will be available to execute the plan.
- Health-care agencies and institutions will be operational.
- A building evacuation plan exists.
- Inefficiencies are expected during a stabilization period.
- Incoming telephone calls will be rerouted within two hours.

A risk management program should reflect disaster prevention responsibilities; ongoing education and training requirements; testing programs; other sound risk management practices; and any additional measures required to support relocation strategies, business continuity strategies, or technology restoration plans. The primary purpose of a risk management program is to reduce the likelihood of a disaster, such as physical security programs, and to take steps that will minimize impact, such as storing computer files offsite, if a disaster does occur.

An emergency response plan should ensure an organized response to a facility-related disaster and provide for the rapid rerouting of incoming phone calls and a strategy for restoring computer processing capability. It also includes relocation strategies, minimum staff required during a stabilization period following a facility disaster, notification for personnel and customers, damage assessment, and media management.

Business continuity strategies, in the absence of other instructions, will be used to maintain business continuity if facilities become inaccessible following a facility disaster. Emphasis is on retaining market share, servicing customers, and maintaining cash flow. Business continuity strategies should have been developed by discussions with department managers familiar with existing business practices and alternative options. These strategies should also include functioning without normal computer support (computer operations may not be restored for days) and with minimum staff if relocation is needed.

COST-REDUCTION OPPORTUNITIES

The most costly mistake that a business can make in developing its plan is to have it aimed at keeping technology running instead of keeping the *business* running (Exhibit 2.5 provides an action plan for cost

Exhibit 2.5 Action Plan for Cost Savings

- Initiate a cost reduction project.
- Have outside specialists (other than those who developed the existing plan) conduct a plan evaluation.
- Focus only on sustaining cash flow and servicing customers during a disaster recovery period.
- Deal with business functions, *never* with computer systems.
- Work with functional line managers and first-line supervisors to analyze options.
- Develop cost-effective guidelines that will sustain vital business functions.

savings). Contingency plans that are not cost effective usually have three characteristics:

1. Plan focus is on keeping technology running, rather than on keeping the business running.
2. No one works with functional supervisors to develop alternate procedures to support vital business functions until normal processing capability is restored.
3. The plan fails to recognize that businesses could continue to function for a week or two without normal computer processing capability.

Cost-reduction opportunities exist due to individual mistakes that alone sound innocuous but, in combination with other related mistakes, spell bad financial judgment. First, an error in interpretation of the Foreign Corrupt Practices Act by accounting firms led to criticizing clients for "lack of a computer disaster recovery plan." That criticism was misdirected. What was actually needed was a business continuation plan to be used in the event of a disruption in normal data processing technology. Placing undue emphasis on computer technology, instead of business continuity, was the mistake. Because the focus was on the wrong issue, it led organizations to assign project responsibility to the wrong department.

Had the objective been business continuity, it might have been assigned to a staff person positioned to facilitate a strategic plan. However, with the focus on computers, responsibility was assigned to data processing personnel, who are normally not trained in the synergistic process used to develop strategic plans.

In many instances, these errors resulted in technical solutions being substituted for sound business judgment because the situation was defined as a computer problem that needed a computer solution. The result for many organizations has been excessive expenditures for redundant processing. Taken over a period of 20 to 30 years, this amounts to millions of dollars being wasted. Exhibit 2.6 provides a brief synopsis of why cost-reduction opportunities exist.

How to Contain Plan Development Costs for New Plans

Minimizing contingency plan development costs centers on five interconnected issues: (1) plan development sequence, (2) mindset, (3) assumptions, (4) communications, and (5) a specialized problem-solving process. If any are missing or not dealt with appropriately, development costs will be excessive, the end product will not be of good quality, and it will take forever to complete the plan.

Plan development sequence means positioning and selling senior management on a corporate contingency planning policy and strategy, and documenting this corporate policy and strategy in writing *before any*

Exhibit 2.6 Why Cost-Reduction Opportunities Exist

- Initial program focused on getting the computer running quickly at costly computer hot sites, rather than waiting a few more days to restore operation at a cold site
- Plan development responsibility assigned to data processing, rather than to a staff position
- Lack of specialized problem-solving process that continually links the low probability of occurrence with the need for cost-effective solutions

---

other activities are undertaken in the plan development process. If this is not the first step, then problem-solving practices are used, which are totally inappropriate. For instance, conducting a "business impact analysis" to determine what is critical *under normal conditions* is unproductive. A definition of *critical* is needed. In a contingency planning context, critical is not what receives the highest priority under normal operating conditions because we are not worried about operating under normal conditions. We are concerned about which business functions will be so impaired as to threaten business continuity following a disaster because they lack alternate strategies to operate under those conditions. What is critical at the time a physical disaster occurs depends on what alternative strategies can be used to support that business function. If a particular business function has alternative methods to service customers for a two-week period when computer processing is inoperable, then there is nothing critical because business continuity is not threatened.

The worst mistake is to begin a contingency planning project by developing a computer recovery plan based on an assumption that the business could not operate for two weeks without normal computer support and that prioritizes application recovery based on the wrong definition of critical as described in the last paragraph. It takes someone with seasoned contingency planning experience to prevail in establishing the proper development sequence. The benefit, however, is that a plan can be completed in 30 days and at a fraction of the cost.

Mindset is the philosophy under which a contingency plan is developed, and failure to document the proper mindset in a corporate contingency planning policy and strategy will result in false starts, lack of cooperation, and unnecessary expense. For instance, the objective of the plan should be "survival," not "business as usual," immediately following a physical disaster because the latter demands ongoing expenditures that annually take away from the bottom line and are not justified given the low probability of a disaster. A more cost-effective mindset is to reduce or eliminate reoccurring expenditures, such as computer hot-site fees and testing, and instead authorize expenditures on an as-needed basis when and if a disaster actually occurs.

Remember that a contingency plan is only a reference document. Managers will decide specifically what to do at the time a disaster occurs, depending on how much damage is done, and what the prognosis is for re-entering the building.

Communicating effectively can have an impact on completing a plan on a timely basis. Repeated communication of corporate contingency planning policy and strategy to senior executives, department managers and key supervisors and to staff developing a plan is extremely beneficial (remember individuals quite often do not comprehend information presented only once). It constantly reminds them of the need to control plan development costs, presents a "road map" that keeps them on the path to timely completion, and acts as a deterrent to a natural tendency by everyone to include too much detail.

Contingency planning for disasters requires a different problem-solving process than is used to solve other business problems because of the low probability of a disruption to business continuity due to a physical disaster. Traditional problem-solving techniques used by most consultants and corporate staff involve lengthy fact-finding studies, as well as addressing and resolving issues in painstaking detail. This is because the problems being addressed will affect the everyday operation of a business. This is not true for a facility contingency plan for disasters. Because it is extremely unlikely that a serious disaster will ever affect a specific site, there is no justification for lengthy studies to gain consensus on what is most critical or for formulating detailed plans. Business continuity strategies need to be documented for all business functions regardless of their relative criticality, and detailed documentation is inappropriate. This contingency planning process is a specialized strategic planning methodology designed to address this need and to minimize plan development costs. See Exhibit 2.7 for a guide to contain plan development costs.

Exhibit 2.7   Guide to Contain Plan Development Costs

- Prepare plan development "road map."
- Assume a mindset to minimize plan development costs.
- Document assumptions on which a plan is based.
- Communicate often to executives and line managers.
- Authorize a plan development process designed to minimize plan development costs and enable a prototype plan to be completed in 30 days.
- Use internal resources to roll out a prototype plan to other locations.

Where to Look for Cost Reductions in an Existing Computer Disaster Recovery Plan

For organizations with a computer disaster recovery plan, there are three areas that should be examined:

1. Plan maintenance
2. Computer hot-site subscription fees
3. Computer hot-site testing

Exhibit 2.8 indicates major areas that should be investigated for cost reductions.

Plan Maintenance. Maintenance expenses are directly related to the volume of material, level of detail, and documentation format. A great deal of "Do we really need to include this?" kind of thinking is required when a plan is under development or being evaluated. If this approach is not taken, issues that should be left out will be included, thus adding unnecessarily to maintenance costs. The objective is to leave out of a plan those issues that can be dealt with at the time a disaster occurs or that cannot be specified until the impact of a specific disaster has been assessed. Remember that the specifics of many emergency response activities cannot be determined until after damage assessment of a specific disaster or incident.

Exhibit 2.8   Where to Look for Cost Reductions

- Plan maintenance
- Scope
- Amount of detail
- Documentation structure
- Backup communications
- The cumulative cost of backup processing subscription fees over a 20- to 30-year period
- Testing costs, including disruption to normal duties

Preparing a quality plan that clearly and concisely addresses only relevant issues requires considerable experience, good business orientation, and a structured format. One problem is that most software documentation packages demand detail that is not needed; in fact, it gets in the way of doing a good job.

Hot-Site Subscription Fees. Backup computer hot-site requirements should be examined for cost-reduction potential. In today's cost-sensitive business environment, computer hot-site and cold-site subscription fees can be a source for large, ongoing cost reductions.

For most organizations, other than banks and communications providers, backup computer contracts with hot-site vendors are a waste of money. They are not needed, because in a crisis such as a disaster, a computer operation can usually be restored within a one- to two-week period somewhere, somehow, and most functional supervisors can find other ways to keep vital business functions running until processing capability can be restored.

Testing. The cost of resources tied up in the testing of backup computer hot-site operations can be considerable. The cost of planning, preparing for tests, scheduling, arranging transportation, testing, evaluation of results, and sustaining corrective action programs can drain an organization of resources that should be used to address daily operating requirements. Failure to formulate a sound contingency plan policy before a plan is developed, to identify a plan development strategy that requires users to be the plan architects, and to select a plan development methodology specifically designed to yield cost-effective solutions will result in a nightmare testing program.

Audit Concerns

Auditors are becoming increasingly concerned about the viability of contingency plans (Exhibit 2.9 lists some of these concerns). Because the data processing department is an organization's focal point of information technology and the department most conspicuously vulnerable to a disaster, management most often looks to data processing personnel to develop a plan. This approach is *not* appropriate for all three plan components:

1. Data center restoration
2. Application recovery
3. Developing "what if" business continuity strategies

Data Center Restoration and Application Recovery. The data processing department should address data center restoration and application recovery; however, the development of business continuity strategies is best accomplished by specially trained professionals.

Developing "What If" Business Continuity Strategies. The heart of any worthwhile plan is the development of business continuity strategies. This requires awareness and education and involves a highly specialized problem-solving process. In most instances, it is not realistic to expect in-house personnel (data processing or any other department) to serve in this role. Effective business continuity planning is not a data processing problem; it is a corporate issue, requiring an organizationwide problem-solving process.

Involving Department Managers

The most serious mistake is to develop alternate strategies for how specific administrative functions or manufacturing operations will operate during a stabilization period following a disaster, without the understanding and support of line managers who would have to use them following a facility disaster. Department managers are the only ones who

Exhibit 2.9   Audit Concerns

- Lack of awareness and education
- Department managers not sufficiently involved in developing alternate procedures
- Plan contains unnecessary detail
- Plan not testable
- Plan is technology oriented rather than business oriented
- Plan is not cost effective

have the knowledge of what alternate strategies might be both workable and practical. They are also the ones with on-the-job knowledge that can be most creative and resourceful in analyzing these options. The way that department managers are approached about participating in developing a facility contingency plan can make the difference between cooperation in searching for cost-effective solutions or protecting their own interests. Most department managers are overworked and have to be selective about what projects take up their valuable time. They focus on getting things done and, as a result, have little time for a strategic planning project like helping to develop business contingency strategies, particularly for a theoretical disaster that is unlikely to happen.

Department managers need to be dealt with carefully and respectfully if their cooperation is expected. Conduct executive briefings specifically for them. Keep the briefings concise, not to exceed 30 minutes. Explain the company's exposure to a facility disaster; explain that such a disaster might affect the company's ability to stay in business and that alternate strategies to service customers and maintain market share need to be developed. Windows of expected outages for: (1) operating without normal computer processing support and (2) the building's inaccessibility should be resolved ahead of time and discussed in the briefing. Never ask "how long could you do without?" because it causes the department managers to go on the defensive, rather than being cooperative because they have no frame of reference (window of expected outage) within which to be creative. This is a crucial step because windows of expected outage psychologically permit department managers to "get their arms around the problem" and deal with it in a positive manner.

If windows of expected outages are not stated up front, department managers will be unwilling to stick their necks out to develop alternate strategies because the problem statement is too broad. Finally, do not ask department managers to write anything down. The individual developing the plan should take notes and summarize the managers' suggestions in short concise statements, with no editorializing or detailing "how" they will be done. The capabilities and judgments of the department managers are adequate, and anyway, the "how" will depend upon the specific nature of a disaster and no one knows exactly what that will be. Business continuity strategies should be reviewed and approved by the department managers. See Exhibit 2.10 for involving department managers.

Exhibit 2.10   Involving Department Managers

- Conduct briefing for department managers.
- Explain exposure to business continuity.
- Describe expected outage windows for computer processing and building accessibility.
- Take notes on alternate business continuity strategies.
- Summarize business continuity strategies.
- Obtain department manager's approval.

NEED FOR COST-EFFECTIVE SOLUTIONS

The low probability of a disaster means an obligation to search for the lowest-cost solution. It does not make economic sense to allocate the same level of resources to solve a problem that has a high probability of happening as one that will probably never occur. If you do not continually make a strong case for this mindset, it will be forgotten, and well-intentioned individuals will select solutions that are sophisticated and costly. It is easy to rationalize expenditures conceptualized in good faith, unless there is an overriding project philosophy to *contain costs*. This cost-control philosophy should be embedded in the plan development methodology so that every solution is examined in search of more cost-effective answers. Assumptions and generalities must continually be challenged in light of the overwhelming interest in *low-cost* solutions.

Allocating resources to develop a contingency plan is a difficult task, made even tougher by the fact that it is virtually impossible to cost-justify how much to spend. There is a big difference between conducting a risk analysis or business impact analysis and cost justification. It can be calculated with reasonable precision how much would be lost per day if a particular production line could not operate. However, because there are no reliable probability statistics on the impact of specific disasters on *business continuity,* completing the cost-justification calculation is prevented.

This difficulty is compounded by the fact that cost-conscious executives are reluctant to commit funds for a *detailed plan* for an event of which the scope and dimensions are unclear, such as a sudden disaster. This is because most plans imply precise logistical and procedural commitments that translate into high maintenance costs. Given the low probability of a disaster and the high cost of redundancy, the goal following a disaster should be to stabilize operations. The real challenge lies in developing cost-effective alternate procedures to support vital business functions until normal processing capability can be restored. Loss of efficiency during a disaster recovery period should never be used to justify spending more money than necessary on alternate business continuity strategies that would be in effect for only a few days.

BACKUP

When a service fails, the primary responsibility of the provider must be *recovery.* The primary responsibility of the user is *continuity of operations.* When there is a power blackout, the consumer worries about how to get along without electricity, whereas the public utility is concerned about how to restore electricity. Similarly, data processing is responsible for a backup power supply should electricity fail. The materials department, however, is responsible for a contingency plan for inventory control if the computer fails, Included in this rationale is the somewhat less obvious fact that users have far more choice and flexibility than the provider. In general, the only strategy for the provider that will serve all users is instant recovery. If that can be achieved, then, by definition, there has been no disaster. The problem is that maintaining duplicate facilities is prohibitively costly.

3

AWARENESS AND EDUCATION

BUSINESS AND ENVIRONMENT

Although all organizations are subject to incited disasters, such as sabotage by a disgruntled employee, some are also subject to disasters peculiar to their business or to their environment. In either event, it is important that senior management be made aware of the specific incidents to which an organization is vulnerable. Consider the following examples: ABC Corporation's centralized computer, manufacturing facility, and distribution center are all located in the same building, one-eighth of a mile from the end of a major airport runway; XYZ Company's major production facility is located within five miles of a nuclear power plant; another company has a major distribution facility next to a railroad siding that often contains tank cars of hazardous material. These situations do not take into account numerous businesses in buildings shared with others who do not practice disaster prevention.

TYPES OF DISASTERS

For the purposes of this book, a disaster is an incident that is

- Caused by a natural event:
  - Flood
  - Hurricane
  - Earthquake
  - Tornado
  - Fire

- Related to environmental problems:
  - Aircraft crash
  - Explosion
  - Localized contamination
  - Hazardous material spill
  - Loss of telephone service
  - Loss of power
  - Strike
  - Water damage
  - Y2K
- Incited:
  - Arson
  - Sabotage
  - Vandalism

Exhibit 3.1 provides a graphic look at the various types of disasters.

POTENTIAL IMPACT ON BUSINESS

Although it is important to recognize the specific types of disasters that might occur to a given company or business environment, it is equally important to understand what the impact might be under worst-case conditions. The process of uncovering these "exposures" is not unlike a long-range business strategic planning process. Most important is that line managers anticipate problem areas, analyze the exposure, and formulate "what if" business continuity strategies that will ensure business continuity during a stabilization period.

Computers

Given the critical dependence of modern organizations on computerized information, it is clear that a long-term loss of processing capability can be extremely disruptive. Although this would not be fatal for most, some sort of business continuity plan should be in place in all organizations. Computers play a key role for many organizations in order processing,

Exhibit 3.1   Types of Disasters

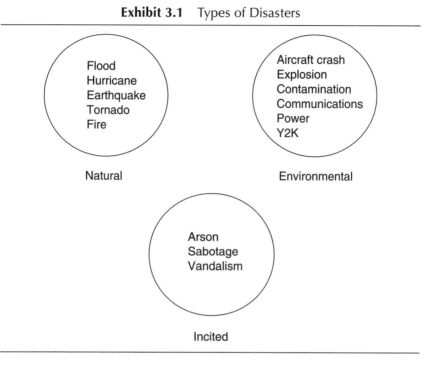

Natural   Environmental

Incited

payroll, work-in-process control, inventory management, billing, and general accounting. Certainly, sound data security and physical security procedures should be in place to help prevent a disaster. In addition, depending on the logistics of a business and the complexity of its computer operations, a more comprehensive business continuity plan may be needed.

Remote Data Communications

Although loss of remote data communications is most likely to happen in conjunction with a disaster that also affects computer operations, it could occur alone. Electronic data interchange (EDI) is increasingly used by customers to enter orders, to check on the status of open orders, and to pay bills. It is also used for order acknowledgment, for transmitting orders to manufacturing facilities, and for invoicing. That is why it is important to have a separate scenario for business continuity in the event that there is a long-term disruption in remote data communications caused by an incident such as putting a backhoe through a communications cable.

Another reason to have a plan that will allow a business to continue operating without remote data communications is the assistance it can provide in recovering from a disaster that has also wiped out computer operations. Although it is likely that computer operations can be restored within a two-week period, it may take several more weeks to reconstruct data communication networks. A plan for loss of data communications will allow remote business units to take advantage of the restored computer operations even though communication lines are not yet working.

Voice Communications

Most people are more dependent on voice communications than they realize, and sophisticated computerized telephone systems are becoming more vulnerable daily. Telephones are critical for marketing, customer service, internal communications, and contacting suppliers. Large metropolitan areas increasingly experience periodic failure in telephone systems. In these environments, some type of business continuity plan is needed in the event of a loss of telephone service.

Vital Facilities

How would a business continue to function if vital buildings, such as offices, warehouses, distribution centers, and production centers, were not destroyed but could not be accessed for several days? Loss of primary work space is the concern. Fire departments, health agencies, and others can order a building to be quarantined because of structural problems resulting from initial disruptions, hazardous material spills, or contamination. For example, recently a small fire in a facility resulted in chemical contamination. The fire was out in two hours, but the fire department quarantined the facility for four days. If a building is destroyed, insurance is the answer. However, if a building is inaccessible or unusable, alternate business continuity strategies are needed.

Loss of Efficiency

Be careful that individuals developing the plan do not *assume* that inefficient solutions are not viable. Quite the contrary! Given the low probability that a disaster will occur, it is important that it be understood that *loss of efficiency is expected* during a disaster recovery period. Functional managers, supervisors, and other employees will be expected to work longer hours and weekends, and vacations will be deferred until the crisis is over.

PLAN OBJECTIVES

To prevent misunderstanding, provide focus, and facilitate implementation it is important to define *plan objectives*. Contingency planning means different things to different people; therefore, the specific focus and scope of any project needs established parameters before the individuals involved can be expected to buy into the process. Once agreement on specific objectives is achieved, the development of project strategy and methodology becomes much less subjective. See Exhibit 3.2 for a checklist of plan objectives.

Safeguard Assets

Historically, in a business sense, *assets* have meant physical assets, such as buildings, fixtures, vehicles, and equipment. In recent years, three new types of assets have joined the group:

1. Computerized data
2. Computer programs
3. Computer processing capability

Exhibit 3.2   Contingency Plan Objectives

- Prevent disasters from occurring.
- Contain the impact of a disaster if one does happen.
- Provide an organized response to a disaster/incident.
- Minimize disruptions to cash flow.
- Provide alternate ways to service customer orders.
- Prevent a significant long-term loss of market share.

Although traditional insurance programs protect physical assets at reasonable premium rates, there is no cost-effective insurance policy that covers computerized data, computer programs, or computer processing capability. The reason for the lack of traditional insurance coverage in these three areas lies in the lack of credible probability statistics on which to calculate risk.

The solution to protecting computerized data and computer programs against loss is to periodically make backup copies and physically store them away from the normal operating environment. Following a disaster, such as a fire, it would then be possible to restore computerized data and reconstruct beginning balances.

Computer hardware presents a different problem. Unlike software, most replacement computer equipment can be acquired from either manufacturers, leasing companies, or brokers. The question is, under emergency conditions, how long would it take to restore temporary computer processing capability? Most management information systems (MIS) directors are confident that, given unlimited resources to get the job done, they could expect to have computer operations restored within 10 calendar days. It is also conceivable that a temporary configuration might have to be leased until a permanent system is delivered. However, the resources saved by avoiding a computer hot-site agreement for 40 years will more than offset the cost of a two-step restoration. A business continuity plan should ensure that there will not be a significant deterioration in either cash flow or customer service during a stabilization period.

Prevention

Preventive measures and detection devices are the most cost effective deterrents to disaster. They reduce the probability that a disaster will occur and help to minimize the impact if one does occur. Preventive steps, such as an annual review and correction program for potential fire hazards, installation and monitoring of physical access control procedures, and installation of backup power sources, are integral to any worthwhile program. Devices such as fire detection and alarm systems, temperature-control alarm systems, and suppression systems (such as sprinklers) are most effective. Their presence, in combination with other sound contingency planning practices, will help to reduce insurance premiums. A risk management program should indicate specific responsibility for prevention and detection procedures.

Organized Response

Immediately following a disaster is the emergency response period, during which are numerous issues that deserve immediate attention. What specifically is to be done will depend on damage assessment and the prognosis for recovery. There is no need to attempt to spell out precisely what will be done in various combinations of events. Rather, it is important to have a list of tasks, such as *media control,* and specific individuals assigned to be responsible for those activities. It is also important that there be some sort of ongoing audit to ensure compliance.

Business Continuity

As stated previously, the objective of a business continuity plan is to keep the business running, not the technology. In this regard, it is important to remember that for many years products were produced and shipped without the aid of computer systems. Systematizing ensured the consistent application of previously established procedures, facilitated the efficient processing of large volumes of data, and stored data so it could be manipulated, sorted, collated, and summarized for different purposes. *Efficiency* is the operative word. However, there is no reason that most organizations could not return to *selective* manual processing or use personal computers to keep track of vital transactions during a stabilization period.

Loss of efficiency during a stabilization period can be addressed several ways. Among the solutions are the following: processing documents selectively and holding specific types until operations are restored, temporarily relaxing processing requirements, adding temporary help to perform increased workloads, and working overtime and deferring vacations until temporary processing capability can be restored. Exhibit 3.3 lists the four ways to compensate for loss of efficiency.

Cash Flow, Customer Service, and Market Share

One of the best ways to determine which business activities are essential, and which are not, is to anticipate their potential impact in three

---

Exhibit 3.3 Ways to Compensate for Loss of Efficiency

- Selectively process transactions.
- Relax standard operating procedures.
- Add temporary personnel to deal with expected inefficiency.
- Schedule overtime; defer vacations and business travel.

---

key result areas: getting the cash in the bank, shipping product, and maintaining customer base (see Exhibit 3.4). Still, because almost every business activity can claim to have *some* impact in one or more of these areas, a qualifying modifier is needed. It is therefore appropriate to define as essential business functions those activities that can have a significant impact on either cash flow, servicing customer orders, or maintaining market share.

Cash Flow. One of the most important objectives of a sound contingency plan is to address the importance of cash flow. But is it essential to maintain the same rate of cash flow as before the disaster? Perhaps not, but it *is* important to *prevent a significant deterioration in cash flow* during a disaster recovery period. There may be several causes for a negative impact on cash flow:

- Manual billing errors may result in a loss of revenue.
- Selective billings may be intentionally deferred until computer processing capability is restored.

Exhibit 3.4 Key Result Areas

- Prevent significant long-term deterioration in market share.
- Deposit cash.
- Defer cash application until normal processing capability is restored.
- Anticipate a severe drop in efficiency.

- Collection activity may be deferred because accurate account status is temporarily not available.

The potential revenue lost to these causes is small as compared with the cost of continuing to provide redundant processing capability over a number of years. Some deterioration in cash flow should be expected and accepted as a legitimate cost of a more cost-effective contingency plan strategy.

The most important objective during a stabilization period is to get cash into the bank immediately, deferring cash application until after computer operations are restored. This can have an adverse impact on credit approval, but because it is cost-justified to defer cash collection for a short period of time, many organizations elect to use alternate procedures to approve credit during a disaster recovery period. One of the accepted alternate practices is to prepare a short list of problem accounts and manually research payment and booking activity in approving credit for new orders. Another is for a business to intentionally relax credit approval for a few days, knowing that in some instances collection could be a problem.

Customer Service. Another area that deserves attention is that of servicing customer orders. During the stabilization period, customer service will be less efficient and the status of work-in-process may not be completely accurate. What does this mean? It means that instead of answering inquiries instantly by calling up a screen reflecting job status, other methods will have to be used. It may mean working overtime, and it will probably mean delays in responding to inquiries. You may have to "hedge" some commitments, but most customers will be understanding if you explain your predicament to them.

Market Share. A third issue is the prevention of a *significant* long-term loss in market share. If a permanent drop in market share is a real risk, then the cost of providing redundant technology may be justified. If a long-term loss of market share would not be the result, then consideration should be given to enduring a short-term drop in market share in view of the long-term savings achieved by eliminating monthly technology backup subscription fees. Exhibit 3.4 highlights contingency planning key result areas.

INSURANCE CONSIDERATIONS

An essential component of a risk management program is insurance. The role of insurance in protecting against loss of physical assets, such as buildings and equipment, is clear. However, using insurance policies to protect against the loss of cash flow, the ability to service customers, or the ability to maintain market share is often not practical. In addition to high premium rates, the primary concern is the inability to prove that losses of this type were *solely* the result of a specific disaster, and not caused by management practices or marketplace conditions. So, for the most part, organizations have rejected insurance policies as a solution to these three issues. However, the extent to which your organization is dealing with disaster prevention and disaster recovery issues *will* affect business interruption premium rates. The following is a discussion of the key elements that affect that rate structure.

Insurance Policy versus Disaster Recovery Plan

The primary function of business insurance is to provide a hedge against loss or damage. A contingency plan, however, has three objectives:

1. Prevent disasters from happening.
2. Provide an organized response to a disaster situation.
3. Ensure business continuity during a stabilization period.

Insurance is intended to provide funds for replacement of *tangible* assets, whereas a contingency plan describes how a business will survive. The presence of a sound contingency plan will have a direct bearing on insurance premiums (see Exhibit 3.5).

What Impacts Insurance Premiums

Many ask the question, "Will insurance premiums be less with a business continuity plan?" The answer is yes. The next question is, "How much will insurance premiums drop if we develop a contingency plan?" The answer is five to ten percent. The last question is, "Specifically,

Exhibit 3.5 Insurance Premium Rate Considerations

- Management commitment
- On-site controls
- Building construction
- Environment
- Business operation
- Inspection
- Sprinklers
- Water supply

---

what do insurance providers look for in evaluating a contingency plan?" They look at eight areas:

1. *Management commitment.* Evidence of management support can be demonstrated by policy and strategy statements endorsed by senior management, periodic memos or letters from senior executives concerning the need to be attentive to disaster prevention, and the presence of an ongoing employee awareness and education program.

2. *On-Site controls and procedures.* Good housekeeping and preventive maintenance programs fit into this category. Insurance agents will observe such things as the presence or absence of No Smoking signs, evidence of ongoing inspection and maintenance procedures, and the extent to which storage areas are free of litter.

3. *Building construction and use-code compliance.* The objective of assessing building construction and use-code compliance is to evaluate the extent to which facilities are in compliance with building codes and the appropriateness of the business to the physical structure it occupies. For instance, insurance companies are likely to charge a higher premium if chemicals are produced in a building originally designed for shoe manufacturing.

4. *External exposure.* The accumulation of dried brush behind a building would be a negative. Similarly, the nearby presence of a

fireworks plant or a facility's close proximity to a railroad siding where carloads of cleaning chemicals are periodically stored would not be good.

5. *Special hazards.* Operations such as spray painting and the use of toxic chemicals and highly volatile solutions will count as a negative. If these are present, prevention and detection devices that help prevent an incident, or at least minimize the impact of one, should be installed.

6. *Supervisory inspection procedures.* A program of periodic inspections by supervisors to verify that procedures for prevention and detection are being enforced counts as a plus.

7. *Sprinkler systems.* The presence of sprinkler systems and periodic testing of those systems in office buildings, plants, and warehouses is important to insurance companies.

8. *Water supply.* Insurance companies like to know that there is a fire hydrant accessible to a facility, and that there is a sufficient supply of water and enough pressure to fight a fire for a reasonable period of time.

Although it may be difficult for an insurance agent to attribute a specific value to each of these considerations, it is certain that in aggregate they will impact insurance premium rates.

HOW MUCH DETAIL?

How much detail should a contingency plan have? The question really should be, "How much detail should be included in a contingency plan?" Three issues will help to determine the amount of detail covered in a plan:

1. Number of different levels of disaster included in the planning process.
2. Adequacy of the education and awareness program.
3. Documentation format.

There are basically two choices when it comes to the number of levels of disaster planning to be included.

1. Address multiple levels, such as a one- to three-day outage, a three- to seven-day outage, and a one- to two-week outage, or

2. Develop one plan for a worst-case scenario, with the understanding that parts of the plan could be used for lesser disasters. With this approach, you will have only one plan to develop, test, and maintain, without significantly degrading quality.

There is a tendency to look at plan development as a procedure-writing project and to include detail normally contained in standard operating procedures. However, the objective of business continuity planning is *not* to write procedures, but to document and communicate guidelines that can be used to ensure cash flow and support customer service until normal operations are restored. Detailed instructions are not needed. If and when a disaster does occur, people are certainly not going to take time to read and follow detailed instructions. Individuals responsible for making decisions following a disaster need only a checklist of tasks that should not be overlooked. It is virtually impossible and a waste of time to attempt to anticipate every combination of disasters that might occur and to specify exactly what steps should be taken in each instance. The important point is to monitor plan development closely to make certain that excessive detail is avoided.

In plans developed by outside specialists, the main cause of excessive detail is the fee basis of their contract. When consultants work on a per diem basis, there is a tendency to:

1. Spend more time in meetings.
2. Write voluminous, detailed reports.

Per diem consulting contracts are counterproductive in developing contingency plans. To reduce a consultant's inclination to provide unnecessarily detailed plans, make certain that the fee is fixed and that satisfaction will be determined by the quality of the solutions, rather than by the amount of detail. Then monitor the data-gathering process to make certain this philosophy is communicated to the individuals doing the work.

In developing a contingency plan, a common mistake is to waste valuable time attempting to document solutions to hypothetical situations that might not occur. Although it is tempting to try to find answers to various combinations of scenarios, this contributes little to the value of the plan, increases development costs, and creates a maintenance nightmare.

ESTABLISHING A FIRM FOUNDATION

The single greatest deterrent to developing cost-effective contingency plans is the lack of an effective awareness and education program. Senior management must be made aware of the following facts:

- The business is exposed to sudden disaster.
- It makes good business sense to have business continuity strategies as a point of reference should a disaster actually happen.
- The contingency planning strategy is to protect market share, cash flow, and the ability to service customers during a stabilization period.
- The methodology to be used in plan development should specifically be designed to yield cost-effective solution.

Department managers need to be informed of the following facts:

- Senior management considers development of business continuity strategies the responsibility of line managers.
- Participation in plan development will not be disruptive to their normal operations.
- Department managers have a responsibility to stockholders and senior management to make certain that, because of the low probability of a disaster's occurring, their plans reflect "bare bones" needs.

KEY RESULT AREAS

A well thought-out contingency plan should: have the approval of key players, be flexible, contain a maintenance process, be cost effective,

Exhibit 3.6   Characteristics of a Good Plan

- Workable—developed by first-line supervisors
- Cost effective—in relation to low probability
- Flexible—same plan can be used for any disaster
- Easy to maintain—keep it simple
- Deals in strategies—not detailed procedures

emphasize business continuity, provide for an organized response, assign specific responsibilities, and include a test program.

See Exhibit 3.6 for a checklist of desirable plan characteristics.

Approval

The plan must be acceptable to internal auditors, outside auditors, senior management, customers, and suppliers.

Flexibility

The plan should consist of strategies, rather than details tied to specific disaster situations, so that line managers have the latitude to exercise judgment when the time comes to implement any portion of the plan.

Maintenance

Avoid unnecessary detail so that the plan can easily be updated.

Cost Effectiveness

Project planning should emphasize the need to minimize plan development costs, redundant backup processing subscription fees, and maintenance and testing costs.

Business Continuity

The plan must ensure business continuity during a stabilization period.

Organized Response

The plan should provide a checklist of issues that need attention immediately following a disaster. It should include lists of phone numbers and addresses of individuals to be contacted.

Responsibility

Specific individuals should be assigned responsibility for each issue that requires attention during a stabilization period.

Testing

Testing with user preparedness reviews and backup procedures verification should be performed at specific time intervals. The plan should state frequencies of testing and document the testing methodology.

CONVINCING OTHERS

Selling is success! If one is to be successful in obtaining the commitment of senior management, the resources needed to do the job, and the cooperation of department managers, the value of contingency planning must be emphasized. Once the persons involved accept the project values, they in turn become sponsors and advocates.

The list of those who need to be sold is impressive: senior management, audit committee members, internal auditors, outside auditors, division managers, department heads, first-line supervisors, and vendors. The problem is that many involved in contingency planning have had little sales training, and yet this is one of the most critical elements of success. If you are able to master *the process of successful selling,* you will succeed where others have failed. Successful selling consists of addressing two areas:

1. Organizational needs
2. Personal needs

Organizational Needs

The first step in using organizational needs to sell contingency planning is to select a specific individual who needs to be sold—the president, an auditor, or another person.

The second step is to classify the sales target as someone who is primarily oriented to *cost, image,* or *business requirement.*

The cost-oriented individual is primarily concerned with cost-related issues. No matter what the subject, this person is interested in items such as cost-justification, return-on-investment, or other cost-related issues. Image-oriented individuals are most concerned with what others think, such as auditors, customers, senior management, and suppliers. A "business requirement" person is primarily concerned with getting the job done.

Although many individuals may evidence more than one of these characteristics, one of them will normally be dominant and easy to spot in most business-related discussions. For instance, ask a department manager to explain his or her long-range department plans. As the manager describes *what* is planned, ask "Why?" Listen carefully: the manager will reveal a specific orientation to one of the three categories: cost, image, or business requirement.

The third step is to select a benefit that will result when the plan is completed, one that is related to either cost, image, or business requirement (depending on the type of individual you are trying to sell). In other words, when addressing a cost-oriented person, select a cost-related benefit.

The fourth step is to ask the sales target to describe the perceived value in the benefit you have selected. It does no good to have sales targets nod their heads yes. The person must explain the perceived value in his or her own words. Therefore, the question must be posed in a structured format, such as: "Can you tell me in your own words why you feel it is important that our contingency plan be cost effective?" The sales target has then been put in a position where he or she cannot do anything but support the project. Furthermore, through the process

Exhibit 3.7   Steps in Organizational Needs Selling

1. Select a sales target.
2. Classify sales target as either cost, image, or business requirement oriented.
3. Select appropriate benefit to discuss.
4. Have sales targets describe in their own words the value they perceive in the benefit you have mentioned.
5. Explain how your methodology will help achieve that benefit.

of stating what is perceived to be valuable, the sales targets in turn sell themselves.

The fifth step is to "close the sale" by describing how the project strategy and plan development methodology will achieve the specific benefit you chose to discuss. The same process is repeated with each sales target, with care taken to select a benefit that matches that person's orientation, either cost, image, or business requirement.

See Exhibit 3.7 for a summary of the organizational needs selling technique.

Personal Needs

Understanding the ego of your sales target can be extremely useful in selling the chosen approach to contingency planning. By understanding your sales target's personal needs, you can then appeal to those needs in your sales pitch, and achieve outstanding success simply because you paid attention to those needs. The following discussion defines six ego classifications and then describes how you can use this insight to improve your selling skills.

1. *Team player.* Likes and values cooperation, is concerned with what others think, likes to serve on committees, and wants consensus.
2. *Recognition.* Values praise, likes to have high visibility, and has certificates or awards posted on the walls of his or her office.

3. *Structure.* Believes in a defined process, is concerned with details, and feels planning is the key to success.

4. *Results.* Thinks that the end justifies the means, dislikes detail, and is goal oriented.

5. *Control.* Likes power, wants to dominate, and feels that no matter who calls a meeting or what the subject is, he or she has a God-given right to do most of the talking.

6. *Low risk.* Attracted to cost–benefit analysis, resistant to change, and likes guarantees.

Selling Process

The first step is to classify the sales target as being dominant in one of the preceding categories. The last step is to make the person feel confident that the plan development methodology will accommodate his or her needs. For instance, when talking to a *team player,* you might say something like: "Susan, I want you to know that I understand the importance of making sure other managers are supportive of our plan, and as we develop solutions, we will review them with others to gain their concurrence."

This process works only on a one-to-one basis. The objective is to make the sales target feel comfortable that his or her personal needs will be addressed as a part of the plan development methodology. This is called selling, and it can be extremely effective in obtaining support, in securing the resources to get the job done, and in marshaling support for involvement in plan development.

EXECUTIVE BRIEFINGS

Concise executive briefings are an excellent way to sell senior management and department managers on overall corporate policy and expectations, implementation strategy, and plan development methodology. However, in structuring these presentations, remember two things: while disaster recovery planning is important to you, executive briefing attendees will have a limited attention span as soon as you mention *contingency planning;* therefore, use bullets and key words in your presentation and refrain from lengthy explanations (or else you will put your audience to sleep); second, tailor your presentation to senior management to focus on corporate policy and implementation strategy, and tailor the presentation to department managers to emphasize plan development methodology. Key components of an executive briefing are:

- Corporate contingency planning policy and strategy
- Disaster recovery life cycle
- Risk management program
- Emergency response plan
- Business continuity strategies
- Corporate concerns
- Departmental issues

Corporate Contingency Planning Policy and Strategy

The briefing should focus on developing separate plans for each facility, including restoring communications technology as well as restoring computer processing capability. It should clarify that business continuity strategies will be developed under existing conditions and will not assume any "planned" safeguards that do not exist at plan development time. Plans can be modified in future years to reflect any environmental changes that have occurred; they should not anticipate planned changes!

Disaster Recovery Life Cycle

Facility contingency plans should only address three time periods; *normal operations,* that is, the time before a disaster occurs; *emergency response,* that is, the first 24 or 48 hours immediately following an incident; and *stabilizing operations,* that is, the period when the building is assumed, for contingency planning purposes, to be inaccessible and the period during which normal computer processing capability may not be operable. Where, when, and how normal operations will be restored should not be included because those issues cannot be addressed until the specific and unique nature of a given disaster has been evaluated. The objective is to permit operations to be stabilized while senior management decides when, how, and where normal operations will be resumed.

Risk Management Program

Although department managers will not be involved in developing a risk management program, they should understand the part it plays in the completed plan. This part of the briefing should take only a few minutes, but sharing it with the department managers will make them feel involved and encourage them to contribute when it comes time to develop business continuity strategies. It should be explained that a risk management program is a combination of procedures and practices, such as physical security measures that limit access to a building and specific areas, which tend to reduce the likelihood of a disaster. It also includes systematic measures, such as storing computerized information offsite so it can be recovered and used after a disaster, which in turn limits the impact of a disaster.

Emergency Response Plan

It should be explained that the emergency response plan covers a time period of approximately 24 to 48 hours immediately following an incident. It ensures an organized response to a facility-related disaster and provides for the rapid restoration of communications and computer processing capability. It addresses issues such as damage assessment, crisis management, relocation strategy, notification, media management, and physical and data security concerns immediately after a disaster has occurred.

Business Continuity Strategies

It is in this area that the cooperation and participation of department managers is critical to success. If they feel threatened that their opinions do not really matter, or sense that their involvement is perceived as superficial, their resistance will harden; their answers will be evasive; and they will not open up to help in identifying options to survive during a stabilization period. Department managers resent data processing representatives assuming the same level of criticality on computerized systems during a stabilization period that they do during normal operations. Remember, although department heads are not willing to give up the benefits of computer systems under normal operating conditions, they can almost always find alternate methods to keep the place running for a week or two without those systems, if necessary. So ask, probe, and listen.

Corporate Concerns

Senior management's objectives in the event of a physical disaster are to do whatever is necessary to service customers, retain market share, and maintain cash flow until normal operations can be resumed. Senior management understands that immediately following a disaster, inefficiencies will negatively impact customer service levels and there may also be some temporary loss of market share and cash flow.

Departmental Issues

Department managers have sole responsibility for determining what strategies should be used to maintain continuity of operations following a disaster. But senior management is also concerned that department managers' time will be taken away from their regular responsibilities to develop these business continuity strategies. Be sure to point out that, to the contrary, a "surgical process" will be used to minimize the amount of time department managers will spend on the project, and that all notes and write-ups will be done by the contingency planner, not the manager. Department managers should review and approve the strategies.

4

PROJECT PLANNING

POLICY AND STRATEGY

In developing a contingency plan, there are a few problems that will be encountered. The first is that contingency planning means different things to different people, and it will be impossible to satisfy all of them. The second problem is considerable disagreement as to which items should be included in a contingency plan. Compounding the first two issues is that there is little agreement on the degree of detail that a plan should include. This is almost a "no-win" situation unless you tackle the project with a well-thought-out strategy and methodology.

LIMIT SCOPE

Which Types of Disasters?

Is the intent to include in the plan all types of unplanned interruptions, regardless of how long recovery is expected to take or the significance of its impact on vital business functions? Should there be an individual scenario for each different type of disaster? Who should be responsible for declaring a disaster?

The first suggestion is to define *disaster* in terms of your own business environment. What is a disaster to a commercial bank may be only a minor disruption to a company that makes soup. It is important to structure a definition so that everyone understands, at least conceptually, what the ground rules are. Predictable incidents that cause minor inconveniences, and/or those that can be corrected in a short period of time, should not be included in a plan, but should be addressed in standard operating procedures. These include incidents such as hardware component failures that are expected to be corrected within 24 hours and most software malfunctions. Plans should deal exclusively with unpredictable disasters that could result in a long-term disruption of operations.

In structuring a definition, it is well to include a time parameter that can be used as a point of reference. One organization described a disaster as (1) an unplanned incident, (2) which results in a disruption of normal operations and is expected to last longer than three working days, and (3) could have a significant impact on maintaining market share, cash flow, or servicing customers. Make certain that the definition is reasonable and appropriate for the particular business environment.

How Wide an Area?

Another question that frequently comes up is, "What about a global or regional disaster—what should the scope of our plan be?" Again, the issue is what is reasonable. As the focus moves from local to regional to global disasters, the probability of occurrence diminishes. Moreover, for many organizations, it does not make any difference whether the incident is local, regional, or global, because they have only one location. If you have only one location, concentrate on maintaining business continuity with the assumption that following the disaster, there will be qualified individuals available to perform vital business functions.

For a business with multiple locations, each facility should have its own plan that addresses localized outages without concern for simultaneous outages at other facilities. Keep the plan flexible and avoid identifying specific alternate locations for business continuity requirements. Although it is acceptable to indicate a *first-choice* backup facility, it is not advisable to "lock in" a single solution without recourse.

Individual Business Units

Contingency plan policy will vary among different business units because they make different products, service different markets, have different operating logistics, and may have different rules under which they operate. Therefore, it makes sense to develop policy and strategy positions at the business-unit level. It is appropriate, however, for corporate management to insist that each business unit develop its own policy and strategy and, as a minimum, to develop business continuity strategies documenting how vital business functions would survive a disaster.

LIMIT THE TIME PERIODS

The biggest problem with disaster recovery plans that never seem to be completed is including too many time periods. The time periods covered should include: (1) before a disaster, (2) immediately following a disaster, and (3) stabilization.

Before a disaster is the only time period most organizations will experience because they will never have a disaster. It is the period that deals with ongoing procedures and practices that tend to reduce the likelihood of a disaster, such as physical security measures that limit access to vital buildings or critical areas. It also deals with procedures that would limit the impact of a disaster, such as storing backup copies of computer records offsite. These time period issues are usually covered in a risk management program and should be included in any contingency plan.

Immediately following a disaster is a time period that normally covers the first 24 to 48 hours immediately following a facility disaster. It represents a checklist of "don't forget to do," such as notification, media management, rerouting incoming phone calls, restoring computer processing, and relocating personnel. It also includes actions that should be considered but might not have to be done, depending on the amount of damage, such as establishing a command center at another location. These time period checklists are normally covered in an emergency response plan and should also be included in any contingency plan.

Stabilization is a time period that starts about the same time as that covered by an emergency response plan but extends for several weeks and focuses solely on stabilizing operations and maintaining business continuity until long-range restoration plans can be made. It contains business continuity strategies for all business functions aimed at protecting market share, servicing customers, and maintaining cash flow. These time period guidelines are normally covered in business continuity strategies and should be included in any contingency plan. This should be the final time period included.

Restoring normal operations deserves no more than a statement explaining why it has been excluded. Determining precisely when, where, and how normal operations will be resumed will depend on several considerations: What type of disaster occurred? How much damage was actually done? What is the prognosis for re-entering the building? Do we have to build a new facility? Only after damage assessment has been assimilated can these decisions be made and a *restoration strategy* approved by senior management. Therefore, a facility contingency plan ends with the business continuity strategies intended for use during a stabilization period. Plans for restoring operations to normal will be developed and approved by senior management after a specific disaster has occurred.

SURGICAL PROCESS

Initial meetings with department managers for the purpose of developing business continuity strategies should be brief, no more than 30 minutes long. Follow-up meetings (one should be sufficient) last no longer than 10 minutes. The review meeting lasts no more than 10 minutes. This means that a department manager is obligated to spend only a maximum of 50 minutes over a period of 30 days.

There are several important "to do's" to keep meetings brief.

First, control the conversation, where it is and where it is going. This is done by immediately—but with respect to the department manager—insisting that you are not interested in descriptions on how the department runs, or why what they do is important, but are concerned only about operating immediately following a disaster. If you do not control the conversation, you will find yourself listening to irrelevant discussions and wasting valuable time.

Second, be sure department managers understand that in formulating business continuity strategies for use during a stabilization period immediately following a facility disaster, the mindset should be one of survival "by hook or crook" and not business as usual. Explain that inefficiencies and delays are expected, some items may "fall through the cracks," and there may be a temporary loss of market share. The objectives are to maintain business continuity and prevent a facility disaster from causing a significant long-term loss of market share.

Third, give department managers time parameters within which to formulate business continuity strategies for the business functions for which their department is responsible. For example, do not say "we need to know how many days you could operate without the computer." The department manager will tell you they "couldn't possibly operate more than two days without the computer." That is the wrong question and the wrong answer. The more correct line of discussion is "we expect computer processing capability to be restored within 10 working days and need to know how you could operate without the computer for that length of time." The department manager will, in most cases, willingly explain how that can be accomplished. Asking the wrong question or asking it in the wrong context can result in causing a plan that should have been completed in 30 days, taking several months or years to complete. That is why it is usually cost effective to pay a skilled professional to develop the initial department business continuity strategies. In following years, these strategies can be maintained with in-house personnel.

GAME PLAN

In determining how to go about developing a contingency plan, it is important to remember two things: first, senior management is more comfortable discussing problem-solving strategies and methodologies than in participating in a problem-solving process, and, second, if you ask the wrong people (senior management) the wrong question (what is critical?), the probability is high that the quality of business continuity guidelines will be significantly compromised. The game plan should be as follows:

- Establish contingency plan policy and strategy.
- Select a plan development methodology.
- Communicate policy, strategy, and methodology to senior management.
- Develop "what if" business continuity strategies with functional managers.

See Exhibit 4.1 for a sequenced list of the major steps involved in plan development.

Exhibit 4.1   Game Plan

- Develop business unit policy and strategy.
- Communicate policy, strategy, and plan development methodology to senior management.
- Conduct orientation sessions.
- Develop business continuity strategies.
- Obtain functional manager approval.
- Document and publish.
- Present to senior management.

Establish a Corporate Contingency Planning Policy and Strategy

There are five key issues that should bear heavily on plan development strategy:

1. There is an extremely low probability of a disaster's happening.
2. Business continuity is the objective.
3. Loss of efficiency is expected during a stabilization period.
4. Functional department managers and supervisors must be the architects of business continuity strategies.
5. The plan is primarily a reference document.

The majority of contingency planning problems, delays, and false starts can be directly attributed to failing to document a corporate contingency planning policy and strategy before the planning process is initiated. If properly constructed, a corporate contingency planning policy and strategy will:

- Contain plan development costs.
- Reduce plan maintenance and testing costs.
- Reduce the number of issues to be addressed.
- Clarify plan expectations.

- Ensure a practical approach.
- Focus on strategies instead of detail.

Because it is impractical to anticipate and procedurize specific responses to an infinite number of facility disaster scenarios, corporate policy should be to immediately stabilize operations with a reduced workforce at an alternate location following a facility disaster. For planning purposes, it is anticipated a stabilization period could last six weeks.

Immediately following a facility disaster, a damage assessment team will evaluate the situation and recommend a long-range strategy for restoring normal operations. This recommendation will be based on: (1) the nature of the disaster, (2) damage assessment, and (3) the prognosis for re-entering the damaged facility. During this stabilization period, senior management will approve a specific restoration plan of when, how, and where normal operations will be restored.

The following usually apply:

- Institutionalize ongoing facility risk management programs that will reduce the likelihood of facility disasters and minimize impact if one does occur.
- Maintain facility emergency response plans that will ensure an organized response to a disaster and document strategies for rerouting incoming telephone calls and restoring computer processing capability.
- Maintain relocation strategies and minimum staff requirements for use in assigning personnel to temporary facilities during a stabilization period.
- Maintain business continuity strategies that, in the absence of other instructions, can be used to service customers during a stabilization period.
- Conduct compliance audits and preparedness evaluations to ensure the continued viability of a plan.

Assumptions, such as the following, are important to be included with a corporate policy and strategy statement to deter getting bogged down in never ending "what if" issues:

- A building evacuation plan exists.
- Qualified individuals will be available to execute the plan.
- Incoming telephone calls will be rerouted to another facility within two hours.
- Computer processing will be restored within 10 working days.
- If relocating personnel to another company facility is required, staff at the receiving facility will be reduced to permit temporary consolidation of personnel. Personnel unable to be accommodated will work out of their residences until office space becomes available.
- Inefficiencies are expected.

See Exhibit 4.2 for a list of issues that should be included in developing policy and strategy statements for a specific business unit.

Select a Plan Development Methodology

To understand why selection of a plan development methodology is important, it is necessary to differentiate between "mechanics" (what is done) and "method" (how it is done). *Mechanics* implies precise steps to be followed. Mechanics is the rote application of programmed machine-type

---

Exhibit 4.2 Policy and Strategy

- Low probability—Explain that it is extremely unlikely that a localized disaster will occur.
- Business continuity—Emphasize the need to survive.
- Loss of efficiency—Acknowledge that inefficiency is expected and should not be used as an argument for spending money on more sophisticated solutions.
- Functional managers are architects—Explain that business continuity is a functional responsibility.
- The plan is a guideline—Not expected to be read word for word, as specific actions will depend on the nature of a given disaster and the prognosis for recovery.

---

operations. The dictionary describes *method* as "a manner of proceeding, a technique." The distinction between these terms is great, and the penalty of acquiring a mechanical program, instead of a sound technique, is a plan without substance.

Benefits of a Good Methodology. Development of a contingency plan, particularly as a contingency against a computer disaster, is not a technical issue; it is a "people problem." *The entire plan development process is subjective.* The lack of credible probability statistics concerning the impact on business continuity of computer disasters makes it impossible to cost-justify how much to spend. You can theorize about how much revenue an organization might lose over a certain period of time, but you cannot arrive at a meaningful amount because of the lack of credible probability statistics. Attempting to find out what is really critical is difficult, because many department managers are reluctant to admit to a noncritical role under any circumstances. Asking, "How long can you do without?" elicits a subjective answer. All through the plan development process, you will be dealing not with facts, but with egos and personalities. Your demeanor in addressing others is crucial; the context in which you explain the purpose of the project is important. Your conflict resolution skills will be continually challenged. Most of all, you need to have good teaching techniques to educate and continually remind plan development participants about the low probability of a disaster, the high cost of redundant processing capability, and the need to look for cost-effective solutions.

The final reason that methodology is the key is that most of the people you will be working with in plan development are not interested in contingency planning. They have more pressing priorities, and they cannot wait until you leave so they can get some real work done.

With considerable experience in systems and procedures, good verbal and written communications skills, and proficiency in the proper synergistic contingency planning process, a prototype plan can be completed within 30 days. The prototype plan can be modified further if needed but at least it will document a solid management policy and strategy for contingencies and solutions for business continuity endorsed by department managers. Additional detail is easily added, and the prototype plan can also be used as a template for other locations.

rojectPROJECT PLANNING

What to Look For. A sound plan development methodology will (1) contain an education and awareness module, (2) address business continuity issues *before* any work is done on restoring computer operations, (3) focus on business continuity rather than technology recovery, (4) include a conflict resolution process, (5) insist that functional departments be the architects of the plan, and (6) avoid unnecessary detail. See Exhibit 4.3 for a description of the major components of a sound plan development methodology.

A Problem-Solving Process. Business continuity planning, a type of long-range planning, works best when orchestrated by a skilled professional using a structured problem-solving process. This process should encourage positive thinking and disallow rejection or negative opinions. By eliminating negative responses, which are a part of many group meetings, energy is focused on building solutions together, and the dynamics of that process is exciting.

Prioritization. A sound methodology will provide a basis to limit scope and thereby improve the likelihood of success. Contingency planning is a broad subject that can mean different things to different people. Some stratification or prioritization of goals is necessary. Because there are limited resources available for this type of project, there is a risk of spreading these resources so thin that their overall effect is diluted. It is more realistic to single out vital issues, such as maintaining cash flow and ensuring customer service during a stabilization

---

Exhibit 4.3   Characteristics of a Good Plan Development Methodology

- Begins with awareness and education program
- Awareness and education continues throughout the plan development process
- Establishes a recovery "window" before discussions with department managers
- Emphasizes the importance of arriving at the most cost-effective solutions, considering the low probability and the long-term cost of redundant processing capability

---

period, and do them well. Most other concerns can be dealt with at a different level.

Communicate Corporate Contingency Planning Policy and Strategy

We can get into more trouble than we think by asking the wrong question of the wrong people. Contingency planning is no exception. To begin with, executives do not particularly like being asked questions by their subordinates, especially questions about issues that are removed from the mainstream of earnings per share. Instead, they expect you to bring problems to them and, at the same time, recommend one or more solutions they can examine to complete the decision-making process.

First, develop a problem statement that describes the exposure and, at the same time, recommends a strategy for addressing it. Managers are not familiar with contingency planning, and your job is to make them aware of its importance and to educate them concerning a plan develoment process. Managers need to understand the low probability issue and the extremely high costs of providing redundancy. They also need to know that although less efficient and unpopular, there are alternate ways of surviving a disaster recovery period that should be considered.

Finally, make management comfortable with your proposed strategy by explaining that you intend to concentrate on maintaining cash flow and making certain that the organization will be able to service its customers during a stabilization period. They will like your project strategy, because you have assured them you are going to concentrate on important issues.

After getting senior management committed to a project strategy, the next job is to sell managers on a project methodology. This is not as important as selling them on project strategy, but if managers are comfortable with what you intend to do (strategy), they will feel even more comfortable if they have confidence in how you intend to accomplish it (methodology). They will also know you understand that functional division and department managers have primary responsibility for contingency planning, that you intend to work through them using a methodology that will not be disruptive to the primary mission of their department, and that you will publish a contingency plan that is concise, easy to understand, and inexpensive to maintain.

Develop "What If" Business Continuity Strategies

The development of sound, well-thought-out business continuity strategies is without question the most important part of developing a contingency plan. It is also the key to acceptance by both line managers and data processing personnel. More important, it is an iterative process that increasingly calls on your skills to do three things well:

1. *Position* your thinking so you can visualize the concerns of individuals; take the time to listen carefully to their concerns and suggestions.
2. *Anticipate* what the problem areas might be and then formulate conceptually what options might be available as solutions.
3. *Communicate* with other knowledgeable individuals to explore the various options and to help you begin to formulate the business continuity strategies that will be most acceptable and cost effective.

TEAM CONCEPT

There is nothing wrong with establishing different task forces to deal with specific issues during plan development. However, the use of teams in carrying out the actual plan should be approached with caution.

I have witnessed organizations frittering away man-hours evaluating, discussing, and debating the use of teams in a disaster recovery plan. I have seen plans that identified no less that 16 different teams, all with specific names, addresses, E-mail addresses, phone numbers, and cell phone numbers, and with notification responsibilities. This seems like overkill by someone who has taken the team concept further than is reasonable. It seems perfectly acceptable to assign responsibilities to a specific individual without any formal team. If that person is not available, then normal organizational default would apply. The important issue is to assign responsibilities to individuals, not committees or teams.

Just as big is not always better, the involvement of more people or teams of people does not necessarily improve the quality of solutions. The first principle is to assign responsibilities to specific individuals, not to a team. A contingency plan covers three time periods:

1. Normal operations (the period prior to the occurrence of a disaster)
2. Emergency response (the hours immediately following a disaster)
3. Stabilization period (the time when "what if" business continuity strategies will be used to support essential business functions)

Emergency response is the only time period in which using teams should be considered, which should be on an ad hoc basis. For the emergency response period, in addition to assigning responsibilities to specific individuals, it is acceptable to identify a team of key individuals with specialized skills. It is best, however, that this team serve at the discretion of a responsible executive, rather than having specific responsibilities assigned to it. Exhibit 4.4 shows the various types of teams that can be formed.

Organization Chart

Even if you are in an environment in which you know reporting relationships, ask for a formal organization chart. You may find some surprises. You may decide in some instances to go around the formal organization to get the job done. Make certain that you have a copy of the formal organization to refer to, remembering that one of the quickest ways to

Exhibit 4.4   General Areas in Which Teams May Be Helpful

- Administration
- Logistics
- Damage assessment
- System software
- Production control
- Computer applications
- Communications
- Computer hardware
- Facilities
- Resumption

damage a project is to irritate or upset key players by not being considerate of reporting relationships. Thoughtfulness, consideration, and courtesy can make up for a world of technical mistakes.

Telephone Directory

Do not start a project without an organization telephone directory. You will continually be given names of individuals to contact for various reasons. A company telephone directory will eliminate the need to ask for telephone numbers and, thereby, increase productivity and help to make certain that you do not misspell names. It may also be helpful if you have to mail documents, as many telephone directories also contain mail-stop numbers.

Auditors' Comments

Before starting a project, it is a good idea to know who criticized what. In this instance, auditor comments and management responses can be extremely helpful in determining project strategy. Instead of asking for only last year's comments, ask for the last five years'. In many instances, this information can provide a more in-depth appreciation for both the auditor's and management's position. The more background information you have, the better equipped you will be to deliver a high-quality product.

PROTOTYPE PLANS

The prototype approach should be considered as a way to reduce the cost of completing a plan.

The prototype plan should include a recommended corporate contingency policy and strategy, risk management program, emergency response plan, and business continuity strategies. The plan can then be easily expanded or modified, as needed, to fit other locations. There are several benefits to this approach:

- A solid "starter plan" is developed quickly.
- The plan can maintained by in-house personnel.
- Cost is minimal.

5

BUSINESS IMPACT ANALYSIS

OBJECTIVE

In conducting a business impact analysis (BIA), it is important to let others know the context in which the questions are asked. It makes a big difference in the answers and will have a subtle but profound impact on the cost of developing and maintaining business continuity strategies. Individuals who usually insist that they could not do without a report for more than three days under normal conditions, might be willing to do without it for three weeks during a stabilization period. Unless time is taken before the questioning process begins to ensure that the mind set is *survival* rather than *business as usual,* the motivation to pursue cost-effective solutions will be missing. An awareness and education program is the vital first step to "set the stage" so that when questions about impact on business are asked, the responses are more helpful in arriving at cost-effective solutions.

The purpose of a BIA is not to document potential loss so that management will make contingency planning a high priority, nor is its purpose to cost-justify redundant processing capability. (See Exhibit 5.1.)

It is not realistic to indicate that a disaster "will result in a loss of $82,000 a day," while assuming that nothing would be done to continue operations. If there is a disaster that temporarily destroys normal processing capability, management staff will automatically search for ways to keep shipping product, They may not be efficient, but they will "give it a go." To assume that managers would "sit on their hands" while their business deteriorates before their eyes is absurd; however, that is exactly the position that many consultants take when conducting a BIA. They are trying so hard to sell backup processing that they misrepresent

Exhibit 5.1   Objectives of a Business Impact Analysis

- Position functional managers so that they are comfortable participating in the plan development process.
- Educate functional managers so that they understand the economics and importance of searching for cost-effective solutions.
- Encourage the evaluation of all options before considering redundant processing.

---

management's resourcefulness to respond and survive under adverse conditions. This can be particularly true of consulting groups owned by organizations in the backup technology business, as well as vendors who offer backup technology and also claim to provide "independent" consulting assistance in business resumption planning. Instead of encouraging clients to develop more cost-effective solutions, many of them sell hot-site agreements.

Another potential problem with conducting a BIA is that we get the wrong answer because we ask the wrong question. Although we must find out what business functions are most critical, we should not ask, "What is most critical?" Nor should we ask, "What do you need to keep going?" or "How long could you operate without?" Instead, it is important to go through a process that will make department managers aware of the extremely high cost of providing processing redundancy on a continuing basis, understand the low probability of a disaster's happening, understand the relatively short period of time before operations would be restored, and realize the need for their participation in plan development. Then work with them to develop "what if" business continuity strategies by asking the right question: *How could you survive in the face of such loss?*

WHAT IS REALLY CRITICAL

The intent behind the question "What is critical?" is to discover which technology should be given restoration priority following a disaster. The problem is that finding out what is critical can be accomplished only as a result of investigatory process.

To arrive at a conclusion, these four questions must be answered:

1. What are the business functions performed?
2. Which business functions are vital, for example, can have a *significant* impact on cash flow or servicing customer orders?
3. What alternative methods could be used to continue those functions during a stabilization period (regardless of how inefficient they might be)?
4. After eliminating those vital business functions for which there are alternate methods of support, what business functions are left?

The residual of this process is what is really critical.

A Word of Caution

It is virtually impossible to cost-justify an amount to be spent on developing a contingency plan. This is because only a small fraction of disasters have a significant impact on business continuity, and there have not been enough of them to establish credible probability statistics for cost-justification. The important thing to remember is that a disaster can happen.

AWARENESS AND EDUCATION

What are the mechanics of awareness and education? This is a two-step process of changing a mindset from business as usual to survival and emphasizing the need for cost-effective solutions, given the low probability that a disaster will occur. Exhibit 5.2 compares disaster recovery period philosophies.

Mindset

Before exploring the alternate methods that might be used to support vital business functions during a stabilization period, it is important to understand that the objective is to do the minimum to stay in business and, at the same time, prevent a significant long-term drop in market share. The key to cost-effective solutions is to make certain that this

Exhibit 5.2 Comparison of Stabilization Period Philosophies

	Business as Usual
Advantages:	• Work 8 to 5 • Vacations permitted • Follow normal procedures
Disadvantages:	• Costs millions of dollars over years • Testing disruptive

	Survival
Advantages:	• Large cost prevention/saving • Business continuity is user responsibility
Disadvantages:	• Drop in efficiency • Use alternate procedures • Overtime will be required

philosophy is in place before the rest of the process is set in motion. Exhibit 5.3 lists guidelines for establishing the proper mindset.

Education

It is equally important to realize that if it becomes necessary to implement these business continuity strategies, it will be for only a short period of time, probably a few days or weeks. This knowledge provides a comfort level to those faced with answering the question, How would we survive? They are much more likely to suggest alternate methods if they understand that the window is small. It is also important for them to understand

Exhibit 5.3 Establishing the Proper Mindset

• Discuss business continuity objectives.

• Focus on essential business functions.

• Look for unique requirements for individual business units.

• Assure functional managers that admitting they could survive a stabilization period without normal technology will not be interpreted as meaning they could do without it on a continuing basis.

that the probability is remote and that the high cost of redundancy demands low-cost, bare bones solutions. Exhibit 5.4 provides information on why education is important in developing a contingency plan.

Cost

There are four areas in which costs can easily get out of control:

1. Plan development
2. Computer hot-site subscription fees
3. Plan maintenance
4. Computer testing

Without a professionally directed awareness and education program as the first module of plan development, the cost containment battle may be lost. Development of "what if" business continuity strategies is a sensitive issue that can move dramatically in one of two directions, depending on the mindset of functional managers. Without a sound education program, business continuity strategies will be inordinately costly because department managers will convince themselves of the indispensability of high-tech equipment. They will insist on its immediate recovery because they will not have been educated on the need to search for more cost-effective solutions and because they assume that efficiency during a stabilization period is cost-justified. It takes a strong educational program for functional managers so that they do not

Exhibit 5.4   Components of an Education Program

- Low probability of a major localized disaster
- High cumulative cost of redundant processing capability
- Need for cost-effective solutions
- Functional managers have primary responsibility for developing business continuity strategies
- Data processing and other utility providers should concentrate on restoring service
- Survival is the objective, not business as usual

assume high-tech equipment to be the only viable short-term solution and that loss of efficiency is to be expected during a stabilization period. If they are not so educated, the danger of committing to exorbitant monthly subscription fees for redundant high-tech backup processing capability is high. Furthermore, testing will be difficult if not impossible, and it will be a constant source of criticism by auditors and an irritant to business unit managers. Simple, cost-effective business continuity strategies need only simple testing procedures. Keep the solutions simple and straightforward.

REGULATORY AGENCY REPORTING REQUIREMENTS

An example of the importance of mindset in plan development is the manner in which information is gathered concerning issues such as normal reporting requirements. The mindset in which this information is developed can play a large part in determining whether a plan is cost effective. For example, you may ask the individual responsible for report preparation what the deadline is for submitting report A to the federal government. The individual replies that government regulations require the report to be submitted no later than the fifth working day of the month and adds a personal comment, "We must meet this reporting requirement."

In this context, it is easy to assume that this report due date will continue to be valid during a stabilization period. However, this is probably not the case. A good example is that in following a major bank fire, the controller of the currency waived such reporting requirements. Never *assume* that regular reporting requirements will have to be sustained during a stabilization period.

WINDOW

A window, for our purposes, is the time period during which an outage is likely to exist. Lack of historical information makes this a real issue when it comes to losing computer processing capability. Most computer directors are reasonably assured that under conditions of emergency or disaster, a window of one to two weeks is reasonable, provided management has authorized monies to restore operations quickly. Vendors would

74

be pulled out of meetings, overtime authorized, replacement equipment air-freighted immediately, and installation specialists would remain on-site 24 hours a day until service was restored. Vacations for critical technical personnel would be canceled, and they would also be available 24 hours a day. Replacement computers would be temporarily installed in any available area, such as the cafeteria, warehouse, or some other space. Air-conditioning units would be placed in windows as needed, computer operators might have to step over cables for a few months, and working conditions would be less than ideal. However, product would get out the door and cash flow could be maintained.

As far as remote data communications are concerned, consider some alternatives. Although we have become accustomed to the luxury of remote data communications, most business functions could survive by using alternate and less efficient communications procedures for a few days or weeks until normal data communication links are restored. Overnight courier services are reliable and available to most locations. They could be used to send inquiries or data to a restored computer operation that temporarily operates in a batch mode. The entries or inquiries could be data entered using hard-wired terminals at the restored site, and responses express mailed or phoned to remote facilities. Although this might cause a 24-hour delay in answering inquiries, it would have no serious impact on maintaining market share.

6

IMPLEMENTATION STRATEGY

TAILOR PRESENTATIONS

Because contingency planning is done infrequently, it is important to review responsibilities for which key groups should be held responsible—before engaging in formal presentations, or discussions. Asking senior management to be responsible for issues that should be dealt with at the department manager level can be embarrassing in any of several ways. Senior management staff will either refuse to do it, will send you in the wrong direction, or may give you a wrong answer. Take time to make certain that you are not about to ask any of the groups discussed in the following sections to be involved in a process to which it has nothing of substance to contribute.

ROLE OF SENIOR MANAGEMENT

Senior management has three responsibilities:

1. Make certain that the contingency plan policy supports the business plan.
2. Insist that low-probability translates into low-cost solutions.
3. Support the implementation strategy.

Contingency planning will always take last place in a competition of priorities. Left alone, it will never be done. Giving only lip service without the allocation of resources to get the job done will result in a permanently stalled project. Contingency planning works best when

Exhibit 6.1   Role of Senior Management

- Approve policy statement.
- Emphasize importance of cost-effective solution.
- Support project strategy and methodology.

chief executive officers issue a written memorandum stressing the need for business continuity planning, place responsibility for implementation on business unit managers, set a deadline for completion, and approve required resources. Exhibit 6.1 outlines the major role of senior management in the implementation of a contingency plan.

ROLE OF A STEERING COMMITTEE

One of the best ways to garner and sustain support for developing a contingency plan is to establish a steering committee (see Exhibit 6.2). The benefit is a group of senior management staff who:

- Endorse the taking of preventive measures to minimize the likelihood of a disaster.
- Agree that steps should be taken to minimize the impact on business continuity if a disaster does occur.
- Recognize the need to establish strategies that would ensure an organized response to a disaster and the ability to stay in business during a stabilization period.

A steering committee should function only during plan development and should be disbanded when the plan is complete.

Exhibit 6.2   Role of a Steering Committee

- Provide accountability.
- Provide forum to discuss strategic and tactical issues.
- Assist in conflict resolution.

A steering committee has three responsibilities:

1. Serve as an advisory group on plan development strategy and methodology.
2. Recommend policy changes.
3. Encourage department managers to participate in the plan development process.

Meetings with a steering committee should always be brief and not get bogged down in details. Meetings should not be held on a scheduled basis, but called only when there is something of substance to discuss. A steering committee should not have less than three, nor more than six, members. Representatives from the following areas should be considered for membership: finance, operations, auditing, management information systems, and executive.

ROLE OF DEPARTMENT MANAGERS

Department managers, important players in plan development, need to participate in an awareness and education program. They are important because they are responsible for approving "what if" business continuity strategies, the heart of any worthwhile contingency plan (see Exhibit 6.3). Among department managers, in most instances, is not the place to find solutions, because they have been removed from the firing line too long. However, their permission and cooperation are needed to work with their first-line supervisors. Never ask a department manager, "What is critical?" The answer, in many instances, will be either inaccurate or

Exhibit 6.3   Role of Department Managers

- Endorse plan philosophy.
- Participate in plan development strategy.
- Orient department supervisors.
- Provide access to first-line supervisors.
- Review and approve business continuity strategies.

incomplete. Nor should one ask how long the department could get along without computer processing capability. They consider computer technology a resource to which they are entitled and are likely to suggest that operating without it for any reason is absurd.

ROLE OF FIRST-LINE SUPERVISORS

First-line supervisors are the key to success because they "know the territory" and are usually willing to listen to new ideas (see Exhibit 6.4). They will take time to understand that redundancy is normally not a cost-effective solution. Their resourcefulness is what you need for success. Take time to educate first-line supervisors about the low probability of a disaster and encourage them to explore various alternatives to normal operating procedures. Encourage them and praise their contribution. Remember that everyone has an ego and likes to be praised for a job well done. Contingency planning is not a technical issue; it is a "people problem," and the effort made to develop good listening and communication skills will pay large dividends in the quality of a plan.

ROLE OF OUTSIDE SPECIALISTS

The traditional reasons for bringing in outside specialists still hold true: your organization is running lean and no one has the time to devote to developing a contingency plan, and/or the outside expert has a special problem-solving process in which no one in your organization is trained. However, there is a more compelling reason to turn to outside specialists

Exhibit 6.4   Role of First-Line Supervisors

- Attend awareness and education program.
- Be resourceful.
- Look for simple solutions.
- Challenge assumptions.
- Evaluate all options.

DEVELOP PLAN WITH FIRST-LINE SUPERVISORS

Exhibit 6.5 Role of Outside Specialists
• Recommend solutions used by similar organizations.
• Provide direction and guidance.
• Evaluate existing plan.
• Evaluate proposed implementation strategy.
• Recommend proven methodologies.
• Recommend quality assurance milestones.
• Provide awareness and education program.

for development of a contingency plan. The reason is the need to educate functional managers on the cumulative financial impact of providing redundant operating capability, and thereby change their expectations and mindset so that they are willing to participate in a plan development process that is not disruptive to operations. Functional managers will accept this educational process from outside specialists, but may be uneasy and skeptical about "hidden agendas" when it is presented by internal staff.

It is always wise to consider independent advice and counsel when confronted with decisions about nonrecurring issues, particularly when contracts that result from such a decision commit an organization to significant ongoing expenditures.

There is another very good reason for using outside specialists to develop business continuity strategies. It is the one-time conversion of mindset that must take place in order for managers and supervisors to make a meaningful contribution to the plan development process. Mindset conversion requires an educational process, which is much more readily accepted when conducted by outside specialists. From that point forward, the plan can be maintained in-house. There is simply too much at risk in hidden ongoing expenses to leave the initial development of "what if" business continuity strategies to untrained staff (see Exhibit 6.5).

DEVELOP PLAN WITH FIRST-LINE SUPERVISORS

Although it is important to discover what is critical, one cannot do this by asking a question. The only way to find out what is critical is through an awareness and education program that positions first-line supervisors to search for alternate solutions, and the use of a structured methodology for systematically reducing the problem to manageable tasks. That is why questionnaires are practically worthless in determining what is critical. It takes a process that challenges technology-dependency assumptions, instills a mindset that accepts inefficiency as a given during a stabilization period, and encourages a search for cost-effective solutions.

How Long Can You Do Without?

It seems like a logical question, but is one that will cause more problems than it will solve: How long can you do without? The stabilization period is a relatively short time. Technology will be restored somewhere, somehow, but working conditions may not return to normal for months. Asking this question puts the emphasis on *inconvenience* and *time* instead of on examining alternate *solutions*. It runs the risk of not adequately examining alternatives, because it permits the answer to be a product of a mindset of business as usual, rather than survival.

How Would You Survive?

It is important to ignore the first response when asking the question, "If you had to, how would you survive without the computer for eight working days?" Most functional supervisors will say something like, "Impossible—everything we do is on the computer, no one around here knows what to do, much less why we do it. All information is in the computer, and it would be impossible for us to function without it."

What you must realize is that, in most instances, the answer is an emotional response and is probably not true. You must be conditioned to ignore that answer and follow up with, "I know, but if you *had* to, how could you keep things going for a period of eight days?" In most instances, a viable solution will surface. The message is clear: if you press hard enough, most supervisors will find ways to maintain vital business functions until lost technology is restored. It is an iterative process of education, anticipating problems, and communicating with the right people to develop solutions. See Exhibit 6.6 for a graphic representation of this process.

Exhibit 6.6   Implementation Process

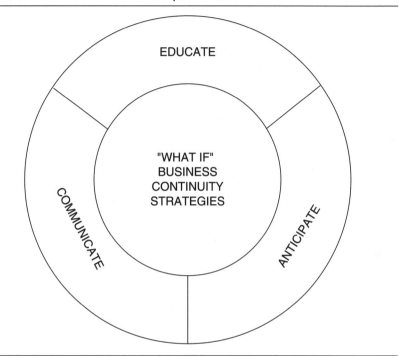

Business continuity strategies tend to fall into three categories:

1. Suspend
2. Use alternate methods
3. Require redundant capability

Suspend.   After considering the high cost of redundancy, the low probability of a disaster's happening, and the relatively brief period before
technology is restored, many first-line supervisors will decide to defer
processing until technology is restored.

Alternate Methods.   Other first-line supervisors, who are responsible for
vital business functions that directly affect either cash flow or customer

service, are able to use alternate procedures to get the work done until temporary processing capability is restored.

Require Redundant Processing Capability. Some first-line supervisors have determined that there is no conceivable way they can survive without backup processing capability and will normally insist that the backup processing capability be operational in a two- to three-day period. The number of functions that fall into this category should be minimized, as they are the most costly to develop, test, and maintain. Exhibit 6.7 shows the three options available for individual business functions.

Industry Examples

Banks and Communications Providers. Banks are the exception when it comes to computer contingency planning, because theirs is a transaction-driven business. They need computer hot-site backup so that they can be operational within a 24- to 48-hour time frame.

A category of business that requires even more responsive computer backup capability is that of communications providers, such as telephone companies. They are expected to have instantaneous redundant processing capability. Most have multiple computers at different locations networked together and designed to pick up the additional load of a failed facility. Because of this system architecture, they do not have exposure to a computer disaster to the extent most other organizations do.

Airlines. It might be expected that if any organizations needed redundant computer processing capability, it would be airline reservation systems. However, most major airlines do not have backup processing capability in

Exhibit 6.7 Three Alternatives

- Suspend processing until normal operations are restored.
- Use nonstandard-practice equipment and procedures during stabilization period.
- Continually fund the cost of redundant processing capability.

the event that their centralized computer facility becomes inaccessible or inoperable. Years ago, they addressed the problem of single-computer failure by installing backup computers—in the same building. Most have still done nothing to provide backup computer processing in the event that a disaster disables their computer operations. The reason is that it is not cost-effective for them to provide such redundancy.

The reservation system is not the airline industry's primary concern in a disaster. The greatest concern is the maintenance system, because if planes cannot be maintained, they cannot be used to move passengers. The industry is confident that they can operate without a computerized reservation system. Although there may be a drop in customer satisfaction and some people will be forced to take later flights, the airlines do not believe this will have any long-lasting impact on market share. It is a smart decision on their part and one that most businesses should adopt. If a computer disaster is not likely to have any long-lasting or significant impact on market share, then the low probability factor should dictate finding business continuity solutions other than monthly hot-site subscription fees for redundant processing capability. The problem is that most organizations have difficulty in disregarding emotions and looking at the issue objectively.

Health Care. Until recently, health-care providers had little incentive to pay attention to cost control. They were reimbursed for costs and had no interest in making a profit. Increasingly, however, hospitals, are now paying attention to costs. Most hospitals could admit, treat, perform surgery, prescribe and issue drugs, and discharge patients by using manual procedures for a week or two. Certainly, nurses and administrative support personnel would have to work overtime to keep up with the paperwork. Within a week or two, however, a replacement computer should be operating and ready to assimilate transactions that occurred during a disaster recovery period.

Manufacturing's primary concern is materials management, production, and shipping. Many times, this means using computer capability to multiple several "like orders" together to eliminate setups and reduce production unit costs, and to later be able to reallocate to specific customer orders. Operating without computer processing capability for a few days means orders will be taken manually and copied for use in production and shipment. Manufacturing costs will be excessive and short-term profits will suffer. In the event loss of access to a manufacturing facility occurs, some options to consider are: purchase items normally manufactured, have suppliers perform assembly operations, lease production capacity at other regional locations, outsource operations, and consider other shop routings. Loss of production and distribution facilities has always been a concern, but they are normally protected by business interruption insurance. Another concern is loss of the computer and critical systems such as order processing and material requirements planning (MRP). Most manufacturing facilities could write orders manually for two weeks and ship from a copy of the handwritten orders. Material requirements planning systems processing could be curtailed for a week or two if necessary; inventory could be intentionally overordered to minimize stock-outs. It is relatively easy to use an off-the-shelf PC program to keep track of receipts and disbursements; the biggest problem is to obtain a beginning balance. One of the more popular solutions is to periodically back up and take offsite a copy of the stock status file. If a disaster does happen, the stock status file is taken to a service bureau and a hard copy is printed to use as a beginning balance.

Distributors need to be able to take orders, locate and pick items, and ship orders to customers. Working for a few days without computer processing capability presents inventory problems, most of which can be overcome with some preplanning. Make believe a computer disaster has just occurred, and it will be 10 days before computer processing capability will be restored. It is obvious that orders normally entered directly into computer systems can be handwritten and that handwritten orders could be used as picking documents. If everything is normally on-line, and there are no paper status reports, the problem is knowing where inventory is located, particularly in a "dynamic slotting" environment, and knowing how much of that inventory is available and how much has already been allocated. These two vital starting points of information could be made available immediately following a computer disaster if data processing, as part of a risk management program, stored a snapshot of the inventory locator file and the inventory status file offsite. Immediately following the disaster, those two files could be taken to another compatible computer configuration and printed as a starting point in resuming operations. Future inventory receipts, disbursements, and allocations could be maintained manually or on a personal computer (PC) until computer processing capability is restored.

OBTAIN DEPARTMENT MANAGERS' APPROVAL

Loss of access to a distribution facility causes other concerns, such as identifying and replacing inventory that may be damaged or inaccessible, and temporarily operating from another location. The snapshots of inventory status mentioned in the previous paragraph will prove helpful in documenting loss to an insurance carrier. The risk management program for a distributor should also provide for maintaining a list of available alternate sites at an offsite location. Drop-shipping is also an alternative.

Insurance companies operating without on-line computers for several days pose concerns unique to that type of business—how to prevent paying claims on policies that had been canceled; how to direct payments to the correct beneficiary when there may have been a change. There are other issues but these are the most prominent. Assume that, even without a computer hot-site agreement, computer operations will be resumed at another location within 10 working days. In many instances, it would be another site owned by the same company, in others a "cold site" where temporary computer operations could be set up quickly. The question then becomes "How do we operate during those 10 days?" Payment of most claims could be delayed for 10 days, which leaves primarily death benefits that should be paid sooner. Again, 10 days is not an unreasonable period to delay payment to ensure "in-force" and verify beneficiary data.

OBTAIN DEPARTMENT MANAGERS' APPROVAL

If care is taken in presenting proposed solutions to department managers, this part of the process normally goes smoothly. Make certain to explain *again* the low probability factor, the high cost of providing redundancy, and the relatively brief stabilization period. In most instances, department managers will approve business continuity strategies with only minor changes. The key is not to be reactionary, but to let the first-line supervisor and manager talk it out. Solutions developed by competent first-line supervisors are seldom reversed by department managers.

Present Findings

Findings and recommendations should be presented to senior management in a meeting of no longer than 20 minutes. Take a few minutes to reiterate the low probability factor and the need for low-cost solutions. Impress on this group that the objectives of protecting cash flow and ensuring customer service can be maintained during a disaster recovery period. Summarize the plan development strategy and methodology. Present a copy of the completed plan for each attendee and *very briefly* review solutions for the top two or three business functions. Thank all present for their support and guidance and be prepared to answer questions. Leave promptly, with the confidence that you have done the job right.

NONCOMPUTERIZED BUSINESS FUNCTIONS

Just as the loss of computerized operating instructions is avoided by periodically storing them off-site in a secure location, similar protection for procedures performed manually is also necessary. The first objective is to guard against the loss of standard operating procedures (SOP) as a result of a fire or a similar disaster. The recommended process for developing alternate business continuity strategies for noncomputerized activities is to:

- Identify all business functions
- Make copies of all processing instructions
- Store duplicate instructions off-site
- Develop an inventory of all documents processed in a noncomputerized mode
- Identify the *vital* information contained in those documents
- Identify alternate sources from which vital information could be obtained if the documents are destroyed or become inaccessible
- Provide backup copies for all others, and store off-site.

Telephones

There have been a sufficient number of incidents of telephone failure and recovery to build a solid case for relying on the utility to restore service in a matter of hours, or at the worst, in a day or two. Utilities operate in the "real-time" mode of disaster recovery; they are always prepared for emergency response and restoration of service. They study, practice, and train specifically for different types of disasters, and they are good at it. Yet there are exceptions. You might want to keep a list of employees who have personal cellular phones that could be pressed into service if needed. Established concurrence on how and where incoming calls would be routed temporarily and how this information would be communicated to customers. Building and maintaining your own redundant communications capability just for disaster recovery is usually not cost effective.

Buildings

The options for planning in the event of loss of vital facilities are not many. It is certainly not realistic nor cost effective to build additional production facilities, distribution centers, or administrative offices just to guard against disasters. The only practical solution for manufacturing and production facilities is to rent capacity from similar businesses until a disabled facility is repaired or replaced. If only standard-practice equipment is destroyed, the choice is either to use nonstandard-practice processes or to sublet those operations to the same organizations used to relieve capacity problems. The usual answer for disabled distribution centers is to temporarily switch demand to another center or to lease public warehouse space.

7

PLAN DEVELOPMENT: THE MYERS PROCESS*

PHILOSOPHY AND METHODOLOGY

The Myers Process is a combination of an innovative consulting philosophy and a unique contingency planning methodology. Its genesis was my eight years with Ernst & Ernst (now Ernst & Young), an international consulting firm, developing and auditing disaster recovery plans.

My consulting philosophy is that per diem consulting is counterproductive and not in a client's best interest. This is because it: (1) encourages spending more time than necessary on an assignment; (2) disrupts operations with many drawn-out group meetings; (3) results in thick and unnecessarily detailed reports; and (4) ends with a staggering consulting bill. Because per diem consulting fees are unexpectedly high for "first-phase" assignments, clients many times, in frustration or annoyance, terminate a consultant's work and never reap any benefits.

My contingency planning work has always been on a fixed-fee basis, which: (1) limits the time spent on an assignment; (2) minimizes disruption to operations with brief one-on-one meetings; (3) includes concise reports; and (4) ends with a consulting fee that was fixed at the outset.

My contingency planning methodology evolved from a market research study of traditional disaster recovery planning practices that disclosed the following problems and weaknesses: (1) using a flawed business impact analysis to focus on what would not get done following a computer disaster, without adequately exploring alternates for maintaining business

---

*Copyright by Kenneth N. Myers.

91

continuity until computer processing is restored; (2) addressing unnecessary issues; (3) documenting endlessly detailed procedures; (4) failing to develop business continuity strategies to service customers if a facility is temporarily inaccessible; and (5) failing to establish reasonable outage "windows" prior to developing business continuity strategies with department heads.

It has been my practice to: (1) recommend a corporate contingency planning policy and strategy designed to minimize plan development costs; (2) establish reasonable outage windows for computer and building disasters; (3) develop business continuity strategies with department heads for operating until computer processing is restored and/or until a facility is accessible; (4) develop business continuity strategies that identify *what* will be done, but allows managers flexibility in deciding *how* things will be done, depending on the specific nature of a given disaster; and (5) exclude issues that can reasonably be expected to be resolved at the time of a disaster, without preplanning.

Why It Has Worked

This process has worked because it is simple, straightforward, and comprehensive, and, at least partially, because of my experience in systems and procedures; finance and accounting; manufacturing and materials control; and consulting protocol with a major international consulting firm. This experience has enabled me to offer a well-thought-out corporate contingency planning policy and strategy; establish reasonable outage windows as a framework for evaluating alternate business continuity strategies; negotiate practical business continuity strategies with department managers; and complete a prototype plan in 30 days.

Creating the right perspective is a crucial first phase in business continuity planning, the stage at which entirely too many otherwise sound plans have foundered. It involves the sensitive encounter of first-line supervisors in user departments. Discomfort, insecurity, even fear, are mixed with their logical and professional responses. If these factors are not acutely understood and carefully dealt with, they can quickly harden into resistance or evasion.

The Myers Process is to deal with these issues in ways that respect both the individuals involved and the delicate structure of an organization's policy. In dealing with first-line managers, it is important to listen very carefully to their information and ideas. They quickly perceive that their opinions count and will play a serious role in evolving a plan.

Once you have gained acceptance and understand the workings of any unique business functions, you can then anticipate specific problems that could accompany a disaster.

In the area of data processing, everything is precise: restore/restart procedures, record lengths, data security, and backup instructions. 94 If contingency planning is presented as a data processing problem, solutions tend to become exceedingly precise and painfully detailed. If contingency planning is presented as a business continuity issue, solutions tend to be less complex.

Once department managers understand that they are responsible for developing "what if" business continuity strategies, they demand answers to some key questions. An important part of problem definition is a prognosis of recovery. Is processing likely to be inoperative for a few hours or for several months? The situation may be likened to one in which someone explains that you are going on a trip and then asks whether you would like to walk, bike, drive, take a bus or a train, or fly. Before answering the question, you need to know *where* you are going. Similarly, users of computer systems are entitled to know, in the event that the entire system needs to be replaced, the estimated time it will take to restore operations.

SETTING THE STAGE FOR SUCCESS

There is a saying among golfers that "most bets are won on the first tee," meaning that negotiating a fair chance to collect after the 18th hole can be the key to winning. Similarly, properly defining corporate contingency planning philosophy, objectives, cost constraints, assumptions, and expectations is essential to timely completion of a plan. While subsequent years' updating can be done by most staff, the initial plan needs to be orchestrated by a specialist experienced in this unique process.

Cost-effective contingency planning does not entail conducting a costly business impact analysis for the purpose of gaining consensus on what computer systems are more critical than others under normal operating conditions. It is a meaningless and costly exercise whose purpose many times is to compensate outside consultants while they become oriented to your operations, or enable in-house systems staff who normally deal exclusively with computer programs, to become knowledgeable of operating methods, procedures, and logistics. A business impact analysis is a carryover from anachronistic large mainframe environments where all systems were contained on one computer and could be restored individually. Today, critical core systems run on a separate computer and are interdependent and cannot be restored individually. If all the critical core systems are restored at once, why is there a need for a costly business impact study? Certainly not to pre-establish what data will be entered first or second, because that is an issue that can easily be directed by the information systems department.

What is critical under normal operating conditions has little to do with being able to maintain business continuity during a stabilization period when the computer is not functioning for a few days. A more productive approach is to present a disaster scenario in which computer processing is assumed to be inoperable for 10 working days, and then let department managers explain how various business functions could be accomplished successfully, if not efficiently, under those conditions. If, under those conditions customers can still be served and market share maintained, then there is no critical issue to resolve.

Cost-effective contingency planing does not include developing a computer recovery plan as the first step in contingency planning. It is counterproductive, based on erroneous assumptions, and can result in proposing to pay costly computer hot-site subscription fees when they are not needed. A computer recovery strategy should be considered only after all functional departments have documented options for surviving while computer processing capability is inoperable. Only then is it possible to know what heroic measures should be taken to restore computer operations in one day versus three days, three days versus five days, and so on. The mistake of developing the computer plan first is usually caused by focusing on keeping the computer running instead of keeping the business running. It is also caused by assuming that while the computer is essential under normal operating conditions, it must be essential for 10 days following a computer disaster. Because many organizations commit the error of developing a computer recovery plan before business continuity strategies are documented, many companies are paying monthly computer hot-site fees and incurring annual computer hot-site testing programs that are overkill.

PLAN REQUIREMENTS

Four objectives of a plan are:

1. Institutionalize whatever steps should be taken to prevent the likelihood of a disaster, including minimizing the impact if one does occur.
2. Document how the organization will continue despite a disaster.
3. Assign responsibilities to specific individuals.
4. Provide for review to ensure compliance.

See Exhibit 7.1 for a list of these requirements.

Prevention

Records retention and computer backup procedures should be designed to ensure that beginning balances and status indicators provide a reasonably accurate starting point for business continuity strategies used during a stabilization period. Procedures for data security and physical security should be designed to lessen exposure to the likelihood of a disaster and to minimize the impact of a disaster if one does occur.

Recovery

Well-thought-out strategies must be developed to facilitate timely and orderly recovery from disaster conditions. Most important is that business is able to continue. Second, whatever processing capability or facility is damaged or destroyed must be replaced with dispatch.

Exhibit 7.1 Plan Requirements

- Prevention—physical security, data security, and the like.
- Recovery—of essential business functions.
- Accountability—during normal operations, emergency response, and stabilization period.
- Compliance audits—institutionalize business continuity plans.

Accountability

Specific individuals should be responsible for certain tasks during the following periods:

- Normal operations (the period of time before a disaster occurs).
- Emergency response (the hours immediately following a disaster/ incident when specific survival scenarios must be implemented quickly, often without complete information).
- Stabilization period (the period of time during which alternate business continuity strategies are in effect).

Audit

To maintain integrity, contingency plans must be audited and tested periodically. Backup procedures should be checked to ensure that proper information is retained and backed up at reasonable intervals. Information should be stored in an off-site location, physically separate from the facility being protected and in a format that can be processed without modification. Business continuity strategies for processing orders and shipping the product must undergo periodic preparedness reviews to examine the likelihood of their working when the time comes for implementation.

PLAN DEVELOPMENT STEPS

The goal is to produce a realistic business continuity plan based on practical business continuity strategies. Evolving these strategies requires a careful, comprehensive process, which involves four distinct steps:

1. *Positioning* plan development participants so that they are in the right mindset to contribute to the development of business continuity strategies that are most cost effective.
2. *Educating* participants on the low probability of a disaster's happening and helping them to understand the low probability, as well

as the high cost of providing 100 percent redundant processing capability, which means that they must look hard for low-cost solutions and be willing to live with temporary inconveniences and inefficiencies.

3. *Developing business continuity strategies* that show how each business function would operate during a stabilization period.

4. *Documenting* strategies in a concise format that is easy to read, easy to understand, and easy to maintain.

See Exhibit 7.2 for a checklist of plan development steps.

KEY TASKS

Focus on Essential Business Functions, Not Technology

Essential business functions are defined as those that have a *significant* impact on either cash flow or servicing customer orders. Business functions that do not fit this model should not be considered essential, regardless of how much users insist they are critical. It is often necessary to have lengthy discussions before agreement is reached to persuade users that a particular function is not essential to maintaining cash flow or servicing customer orders. An activity that makes order processing more efficient is not important, nor is the argument that information is needed for a report. Reports can be reconstructed after the fact. The important functions are to deposit cash and to ship product.

Exhibit 7.2   Plan Development Steps

- Positioning—Make participants feel comfortable with the plan development methodology.
- Education—Help participants develop the proper perspective.
- Develop flexible "what if" business continuity strategies.
- Documentation and publishing—Keep it concise and easy to understand.

Protect Ongoing Needs

Users are often reluctant to admit that they could do without certain systems during a stabilization period because they are concerned that their admission might be construed to mean that such systems are not needed during normal operations and could be eliminated.

Emphasize the Low Probability of a Major Disaster

Most managers will never be involved in a major disaster; minor operating inconveniences, perhaps, but not a major long-term outage. It is important to emphasize continually the *extremely* low probability of a major disaster.

Link Low Probability with the Need for
Low-Cost, Simple Solutions

It is important to emphasize repeatedly the low probability of a disaster and to remind department managers that they have a responsibility to search for "what if" business continuity strategies.

Analyze Alternate Business Continuity Strategies

It is helpful to have a list of possible alternate strategies in hand before meeting with users. Take time, in a relaxed atmosphere, to help users brainstorm possible conceptual solutions without worrying about how they might be accomplished. Many times, you will end up taking parts of one idea and combining it with another to arrive at a final solution. Unless you go through the process of airing conceptual solutions in a nonthreatening environment, they may never surface. See Exhibit 7.3 for a list of issues that should be covered during this process.

DEVELOPING "WHAT IF" BUSINESS
CONTINUITY STRATEGIES

The development of alternate operating strategies requires analyzing technology dependencies in detail, observing unique operating characteristics,

Exhibit 7.3   Phase I—Key Tasks

- Identify vital record required to support essential business functions.
- Identify processing requirements necessary to maintain cash flow and service customers.
- Evaluate alternate management practices.
- Identify key management reports.
- Identify systems support personnel.
- Identify primary users.
- Develop business continuity strategies.

---

and identifying essential processing requirements. This is a highly specialized process that continually stresses the importance of concentrating on essential business functions and vital records.

Identify Vital Records

During a stabilization period, the concern is not with systems, but only with vital records. Most systems contain 85 percent extraneous data that is not essential to survival for short periods of time. This is why it is counterproductive to discuss systems with users. Instead, discussion should be limited to vital records because they constitute the bottom line. If users start to talk in terms of systems, then the discussion must be directed back to vital records. *In no instance should a system be the focus.* Systems are a luxury; vital records are a necessity.

Evaluate Alternate Operating Strategies

Management practices often become dependent on computer systems to the extent that it is hard to think of operating otherwise. However, this issue must be addressed because the use of different management techniques can often compensate for lack of systems support. Department managers should be encouraged to think of methods that could be used temporarily.

Finalize Alternate Business Continuity Strategies

The ultimate goal is to develop alternate business continuity strategies that describe how essential business functions will operate until lost work space or technology is restored. Alternate business continuity strategies reflect alternate management practices that department heads are willing to invoke for a short period of time, the acceptance of a temporary loss of efficiency, and a focus only on business functions that have a direct bearing on either cash flow or customer service. See Exhibit 7.4 for a list of activities that should be covered.

Obtain Department Managers' Approval of Alternate Business Continuity Strategies

Department managers must approve the finished product. Input will need editing for consistency in the amount of detail and style of presentation across all business functions. Asking individual departments

Exhibit 7.4   Phase II—Key Tasks

- Encourage users to accept primary responsibility for business continuation planning.
- Document exposure to disaster situations.
- Review departmental use of computer systems.
- Review backup procedures.
- Review systems level documentation.
- Document computer hardware specifications.
- Document teleprocessing network specifications.
- Evaluate the risk to essential business functions.
- Analyze alternate strategies to serve customers and support essential business functions during a stabilization period.

to document their own strategies may seem logical, but continuity and compatibility may be lacking. Department managers should formulate and be the architects of "what if" business continuity strategies, but *one individual* should control the documentation process. When you think it is presentable, make an appointment with the department manager and review it in as much detail as required. Ask for additions, changes, or corrections; this process will tend to give the department managers ownership in the finished product.

COMPUTER PROCESSING ALTERNATIVES

The following are examples of "what if" business continuity strategies:

Accounts Payable

Strategy
- Match receiving reports to invoices manually.
- Selectively approve invoices with large discounts.
- Defer other payments until computer processing capability is restored.
- Prepare checks manually.

Accounts Receivable

Strategy
- Prepare a "short list" of problem credit accounts; manually analyze and approve credit.
- Automatically approve other orders from existing customers up to a specified limit.
- Approve new customer orders manually.
- Apply cash after computer processing capability is restored.

Billing

Strategy
- Invoice large dollar amounts manually.
- Defer other invoicing until computer processing capability is restored.

Cost Accounting

Strategy
- Collect raw cost accounting data manually.
- Prepare cost accounting reports after computer processing capability is restored.

Customer Service

Strategy
- Refer to the latest hard copy of job status.
- Explain to customers that the computer system is down, but that you will check the status of their orders and call them back.
- Use standard production times for standard products and consult experienced process control personnel for estimated delivery times for special orders.

Engineering

Strategy
- Use aperture cards to view engineering change orders.
- Process changes manually that will have an impact on work-in-process.
- Implement critical work-in-process changes manually.

Fixed Assets

Strategy
- Maintain manual log of transactions during the interim processing period.

- Update records and prepare reports when computer processing capability is restored.

General Ledger

Strategy
- Obtain copies of the most recent financial statements.
- If an outage occurs during the closing cycle, use top-line estimates to close the books or defer closing until computer processing capability is restored.

Human Resources

Strategy
- Defer employee status and salary changes until computer processing capability is restored.
- Make retroactive salary adjustments after computer processing capability is restored.

Inventory Management

Strategy
- Use a computer service bureau to print a copy of the prior day's computer record of inventory status.
- Use a PC spreadsheet to maintain a net balance of inventory receipts and disbursements during the interim processing period.
- Intentionally overorder "B" and "C" items to prevent stock-outs. Plan to work off excess inventory later.
- Monitor and reorder "A" items manually.
- Update computer records for transactions during the stabilization period.

Material Requirements Planning

Strategy
- Operate using the latest hard-copy master schedule, making selected adjustments manually.

- Intentionally overorder "B" and "C" items with the expectation of working off excess inventory later.
- Manually review the impact of new requirements and changes, and selectively order additional "A" items as deemed necessary.

Order Processing

Strategy
- Use fax or phone to receive electronic data interchange (EDI) orders.
- Write new orders manually.
- Prepare copies for order picking or production scheduling.
- Copy and mark up previous order routings for similar orders.
- Use the latest copy of order status report combined with actual shop floor visits to update the status of work-in-process.

Payroll

Strategy
- Store the most recent backup copy of payroll check images offsite.
- Obtain the latest copy of payroll check images and use local computer utility to produce duplicate copies of those checks.
- Prepare checks for new hires and remove checks for terminations manually.
- Include a notice with payroll checks indicating that shortages or averages will be corrected after normal processing capability is restored.

Production Scheduling

Strategy
- Obtain the latest hard copy of the master schedule and the detailed production schedule.
- Prepare move tickets manually as needed.
- Manually update the latest detailed production schedule.

Purchasing

Strategy
- Update the latest hard copy of material status manually.
- Prepare purchase orders manually.
- Prepare copies of purchase orders for receiving.
- Expedite manually.

Receiving

Strategy
- If necessary, use "no P.O." (purchase order) procedures to receive material.
- Use a copy of the packing list to document receipt.
- Record receipts manually on a backup form.
- Send a copy of each receipts form to accounts payable for approval of invoices.

Shipping

Strategy
- Use a copy of the order to set up transportation.
- Prepare bills of lading manually.
- Use similar prior shipment records to develop routing.

DOCUMENTATION

Documentation review and publishing constitute the next phase. This involves translating alternate business continuity strategies into a plan tailored to the operating needs of an organization (see Exhibit 7.5). The objective is to produce a concise deliverable document that can be easily used as a reference should an actual disaster occur. The following are recommended section headings for a plan, with suggested wording to serve as a starting point.

Exhibit 7.5   Plan Documentation Sections

- Policy
- Strategy
- Executive summary
- Risk management program
- Emergency response plan
- Business continuity strategies

Policy

The objectives of a contingency plan are to provide an organized response to an isolated disaster that would render communications, computers, or facilities inoperable or inaccessible, and to prevent a significant deterioration in either cash flow or our ability to service customer orders during a stabilization period.

Strategy

The strategy of a contingency plan is to:

- Ensure that all relevant computerized software and data bases are duplicated and stored in a secure off-site location for use in recovery.
- Provide alternate processing strategies to support key business functions and maintain market share during a stabilization period.
- Publish an organized plan that can be used as a reference should a disaster actually occur.
- Address environmental and systems changes.

See Exhibit 7.6 for an example of policy and strategy.

Exhibit 7.6   Policy and Strategy—Examples

Policy

The contingency plan policy of the Industrial Foods Division is to (1) ensure an organized and effective response to an isolated disaster that would render telephone communications, remote data communications, and/or computer equipment inaccessible or inoperative, or normal work locations inaccessible, and (2) ensure business continuity for business functions dependent on computer technology until normal processing capability is restored.

Strategy

The strategy of the Industrial Foods contingency plan is as follows:

1. Ensure that all relevant computer software and data bases are duplicated and stored in a secure off-site location for use in recovery.
2. Provide alternate processing strategies to support essential business functions and maintain cash flow during a computer disaster recovery period.
3. Publish an organized plan that can be used as a reference should a disaster actually occur.
4. Identify responsibility to restore voice communications in the event of a loss of telephone service.
5. Provide for plan maintenance for environmental and systems changes.

Executive Summary

This contingency plan is primarily designed to protect against the sudden loss of telephone service, computer processing capability, or access to vital facilities. A disaster might be caused by an incident such as accidental fire, arson, contamination by hazardous material, aircraft accident, tornado, or earthquake. Experience indicates the probability of such a disaster's occurring at a given installation is extremely remote. However, owing to present and planned dependency on technology and vital facilities, "what if" business continuity strategies have been developed to protect market share and to ensure that critical business functions can continue to operate until processing capability is restored.

Exhibit 7.7 Executive Summary

The Industrial Foods Division disaster recovery and business continuation plan is designed to protect against the sudden loss of telephone communications, data communications, and/or computer processing capability through disasters such as fire, water, explosion, aircraft accident, or sabotage. Experience indicates that the probability that such a disaster might occur to a given installation is extremely remote. However, owing to present and planned dependency on computer processing, Interim Processing strategies and guidelines have been developed to protect market share and to ensure that critical business functions can continue to operate until processing capability is restored.

It is expected that computer operations will be able to be restored within eight working days. In a worst-case scenario, these interim processing strategies could be in effect longer. Although temporary discontinuance of some systems may result in a loss of efficiency, the objective is to prevent a significant deterioration in cash flow and/or the ability to service customers during a disaster recovery period.

It is expected that computer operations will be restored within a one- to two-week period. In a worst-case scenario, these business continuity strategies could be in effect longer. Although temporary discontinuance of some systems may result in a loss of efficiency, the objective is to prevent a significant deterioration in cash flow and/or the ability to service customers during a stabilization period.

See Exhibit 7.7 for an example of an executive summary.

Risk Management Program

This phase of the plan addresses normal operating practices that will be followed to provide an accurate and timely starting point should original data be lost or destroyed. It assigns direct responsibility for specific actions that should be institutionalized into existing position descriptions. The risk management program section also provides for periodic testing of alternate business continuity strategies capability.

See Exhibit 7.8 for an example of a risk management program.

Exhibit 7.8   Risk Management Program—Examples

Risk management programs outline tasks and responsibilities necessary to support and maintain an effective ongoing disaster recovery and business continuation plan, before a localized disaster occurs.

Responsibility	*Action*
Operations Manager	Ensure that all relevant files and data bases are consistently backed up in accordance with the processing frequency indicated on application data sheets.
Senior Operator	Rotate magnetic tapes representing data bases and data sets based on existing daily, weekly, and monthly schedules to the off-site location.
Operations Manager	Store source programs, compiled programs, operating systems, data communication, and related system software at the off-site location.
	Maintain up-to-date documentation to support production scheduling and computer operations at the off-site location.
	Maintain current applications data entry procedures and program documentation at the off-site location.

Emergency Response Plan

Although a thorough analysis of operating needs has categorized systems into critical and noncritical categories, the specifics of a recovery program can be determined only at the time of an actual disaster. This depends on the nature of the disaster, the point in time when the disaster occurs, and the anticipated period of disruption. Plan activation and definition require a global knowledge of management information systems (MIS) and control of system support resources. The emergency response section identifies required tasks and responsibilities, such as ordering replacements for damaged equipment and coordinating user processing activities.

See Exhibit 7.9 for an example of an emergency response plan.

Exhibit 7.9	Emergency Response Plan

An emergency response plan identifies required tasks and responsibilities that must be addressed at the time a specific disaster occurs or are needed to establish temporary data processing capability at another location. It contains actions assigned to specific individuals as well as to an emergency response team who may perform individually or collectively during the stabilization period, at the discretion of the information systems manager.

Responsibility	*Action*
Information Systems Manager	Determine whether the disaster recovery and business continuation plan will be activated. Notify appropriate personnel.
Operations Manager	Initiate any reconstruction that might be required at a temporary data processing location.
	Document a chronological list of all key events surrounding the disaster emergency response actions and interim processing activities.
	Instruct user department managers to execute plans for implementing business continuity strategies.
	Notify proper authorities, such as police and fire department, based on the nature of the disaster.
	Expedite installation of new telephone/communications systems as required.

Stabilization Period

The stabilization period represents the time during which business continuity strategies will be used to protect market share and provide support to vital business functions.

1. Profile

- *System or functional name.* Gives the name of the business function or system being addressed.

- *System or functional description.* Includes a description of the highlights and major activities of the business function or computer system being addressed.
- *Key reports.* Lists the major reports used to administer the specific activity.
- *Inquiry capability.* Highlights the need to access information for either customer or management needs.
- *Dependencies.* Reflects other business functions or systems that are normally dependent on input from this activity.

See Exhibit 7.10 for an example of a profile section.

2. *"What if" Business Continuity Strategies*

- *Startup.* Indicates steps that need to be taken to make the transition from "business as usual" processing to "alternate methods" processing during a stabilization period.

Exhibit 7.10   Systems Profile—Example

System name: Accounts Payable

System description:

This system facilitates vouchering of approved invoices and check processing. The system also permits on-line generation of checks for COD deliveries.

Key reports:

Checks

Check register

Transaction log

On-line inquiry capability:

Invoice status

Applications dependent on output from this system:

General ledger

Purchasing

- *Interim processing.* Highlights activities that need to be done to support the alternate processing methods. Specifically *how* they will be performed is not to be included as long as the functional manager is confident that those details can be easily worked out when they are needed.
- *Records retention.* Indicates those transactions that should be saved so that computer data bases can be updated when normal processing capability is restored.

See Exhibit 7.11 for an example of business continuity strategies.

Exhibit 7.11   Business Continuity Strategies—Example

System name: Accounts Payable

Business continuity strategies highlight activities to be addressed in support of Interim Processing strategies. Following are the business continuity strategies for this system:

A. Startup

The following steps should be taken in anticipation of implementing business continuity strategies:

- Instruct plant and mill locations to pay grain invoices manually.

B. Interim Processing

The following are processing strategies that will be in effect until normal computer processing is restored:

- Accounts payable pays selected vendor invoices manually to maximize discount allowances.
- Trader offices prepare vendor checks manually.

C. Restoration of computerized data

Records of the following business transactions should be retained so that data files can be updated when normal computer processing is restored:

- Manual checks

Maintenance, Preparedness Reviews, and Testing

Because contingency plans are environmentally dependent, effective maintenance, periodic preparedness reviews, and testing are important. Their purpose is to:

- Ensure viability of alternate business continuity strategies through an ongoing awareness and education program and periodic preparedness evaluations.
- Update and maintain contingency plans for systems changes, hardware upgrades, and assigned responsibilities.
- Test backup computer processing capability.

COST BENEFITS

The cost benefits attributable to this process for plan development are primarily the result of the awareness and education module that precedes the business impact analysis. Most other "methodologies" use a business impact analysis to justify the cost of unneeded redundant computer processing capability. This process uses awareness and education to instill in the minds of functional managers the need to search for the most cost-effective solutions. Cost benefits fall into five categories:

1. Lower plan development cost.
2. Lower backup communications cost.
3. Minimization/avoidance of backup computer subscription fees.
4. Lower plan maintenance cost.
5. Lower testing cost.

Lower Plan Development Costs

The cost of developing a contingency plan is directly related to the plan development strategy. If you fail to contain scope; complete the business continuity plan before working on a data processing plan; determine in advance how much detail is appropriate; conduct an awareness and education program before performing a business impact risk analysis; or insist that first-line supervisors be the architects of business continuity strategies, then costs will soar unnecessarily and the quality of the deliverable document will be greatly compromised.

Lower Backup Communications Costs

In the "business as usual" mindset, on-line telecommunications capability is indispensable. In the "survival" mindset, it is a luxury. The key is the implementation of an awareness and education program *before* a risk analysis is conducted, so that answers and solutions are pursued within the proper mindset. Ask remote computer users the right question: "If the computer were operational, but data communications lines were not working, how could you continue to operate?" Although it would be inconvenient and inefficient, most users would come to the conclusion that they *could* use either telephones, fax machines, or overnight mail to submit and receive system inquiries. This can avoid the necessity of installing and maintaining backup data communications network capability in the event of a communications failure. It will also help to get remote users back on their feet following a computer disaster during which hardware is operational but the restoration of the communications network may take a few more weeks.

Minimization/Avoidance of Back-up Computer Subscription Fees

Most MIS directors are reasonably confident that, given unlimited resources to expedite delivery, authorization to schedule overtime work, and a designated location where they would be permitted to install temporarily a replacement computer, they could restore a mainframe computer operation within a 5- to 10-day period. This extremely important information should be communicated to users during the awareness and education program before conducting a risk analysis. Without this information, users may insist that they could not go more than three days without computer processing. The key to avoiding excessive backup computer subscription fees is to define the "window" *first*. Unless users have this information, their responses to the questions, "What is critical?" "How long can you do without?" or "What do you need?" can result in backup computer subscription fees that could have been avoided.

Lower Plan Maintenance Costs

Lower plan maintenance cost is really a function of avoiding unnecessary detail, because the more detail a plan contains, the more costly it is to maintain. Be skeptical of computerized business continuity planning programs, as most encourage an inordinate amount of unnecessary detail. Internal auditors are aware that excessive detail is the downfall of many plans. No one reads such plans; they are not maintained; and organizations have to redo these plans every three to five years. Keep it simple, avoid unnecessary detail, and the plan will live—with less maintenance.

Lower Testing Costs

The simpler the plan, the lower the testing cost. Complicated business continuity strategies force unnecessarily complex testing programs. The results are usually frustrating and depressing. Testing is emphasized because auditors know users have little knowledge of what their responsibilities would be during a stabilization period. As a result, auditors insist on testing as a way to force user involvement. The need to test or to periodically examine the viability of proposed business continuity strategies will never be completely eliminated. However, auditors' insistence on testing will decrease once they discover that users are the architects of a plan. See Exhibit 7.12 for a list of cost benefits.

CORPORATE BENEFITS

Two benefits of the plan development process are that it produces a business solution rather than a technical one, and it encourages functional

Exhibit 7.12   Cost Benefits

- Lower plan development cost.
- Lower backup communications cost.
- Minimization/avoidance of computer hot-site/cold-site subscription fees.
- Lower plan maintenance cost.
- Lower testing cost.

managers to accept responsibility for contingency planning. These corporate benefits fall into four categories:

1. Sound strategy for plan development.
2. Focus is on keeping the business running.
3. Auditors are supportive.
4. Resolves what is critical.

Sound Strategy for Plan Development

The primary reason that many organizations do not adequately address a contingency plan is that it represents unfamiliar territory. They are not comfortable looking into the abyss. When executives are uncomfortable about an issue, they tend to find a rationale for delaying action. They are particularly reluctant to commit significant resources to a *detailed plan* for an event of which the scope and dimensions are unclear. If you make it clear that your strategy is to make certain that the window is realistic, that the plan will concentrate only on business functions that have a significant impact on cash flow and servicing customer orders, and that the intent is to avoid unnecessary detail, then executives will feel comfortable and be supportive.

Focus Is on Keeping the Business Running

Although the need to recover technology is understood, the importance of documenting how business continuity will be maintained during a stabilization period is the primary purpose of a plan. The Myers Process continually focuses on business continuity and uses essential business requirements to prioritize recovery operations.

Auditors Are Supportive Sponsors

Directors of internal audit are supportive of the Myers Process development plan described here, not only because it focuses on business continuity and solves the problem at the business unit level, but because it also emphasizes the avoidance of unnecessary detail. Directors of

Exhibit 7.13 Corporate Benefits

- Sound strategy for plan development.
- Focus is on keeping the business running.
- Internal auditors are supportive sponsors.
- Ensures business continuity until temporary processing capability is restored.
- Ensures business continuity between the time temporary processing is restored and the time when communications networks are operational.
- Resolves what is really critical.

internal audit know that excessive detail discourages maintenance and causes a plan to become obsolete before its time.

Resolves What Is Critical

The only way to determine what is critical is to guide users through a process that presents a reasonable window of outage and forces analysis and selection of cost-effective options to support vital business functions until temporary processing capability can be restored. The residual of that process is what is critical. Questionnaires are ineffective in determining what is critical, because of the absence of a sound problem-solving process. See Exhibit 7.13 for a list of corporate benefits.

8

MAINTENANCE, EDUCATION, AND TESTING

OBJECTIVES

Because contingency plans are environmentally dependent, effective maintenance, continuing education, and preparedness reviews are needed. Their purpose is to:

- Ensure viability of "what if" business continuity strategies through a program of continuing education and preparedness evaluation.
- Update and maintain contingency plans for systems changes, hardware upgrades, and assigned responsibilities.
- Test backup technology.

MAINTENANCE

Systems and procedural changes should be reviewed quarterly to ensure that new customer services or modifications to existing services have not invalidated alternative business continuity strategies. They should be reviewed with data processing personnel to make certain that computer recovery plans are compatible with these strategies.

Reviews should also be conducted to ensure awareness of data processing responsibilities during normal operations, emergency response, and stabilization periods.

Normal Operations

Activities included in the normal operations section form the foundation on which much of the plan is based. There is a great deal of dependency on this section. Annual reviews should be scheduled to examine and update procedures and personnel assignments to prevent the plan from deteriorating and becoming obsolete.

Emergency Response

An annual meeting should be scheduled to ensure that promotions and attrition have not affected assigned responsibilities.

"What If" Business Continuity Strategies

Business continuity strategies should be reviewed annually to ensure that new customer services or modifications to existing services have not invalidated these strategies. The business continuity strategies should in turn be reviewed with the data processing department to make certain that computer processing continues to be compatible with capacities and capabilities.

CONTINUING EDUCATION AND PREPAREDNESS REVIEWS

To ensure that a plan is workable, individuals need to be aware of their responsibilities and prepared to implement them in the event of a disaster. Through a continuing program of education, periodic preparedness review, and evaluation, user awareness can be maintained.

On a selected basis, functional departments should be examined to determine how prepared they are to cope with an actual disaster. The examination should include, but not necessarily be limited to, the following considerations:

- Awareness of the plan.
- Accessibility of a copy of the plan at an off-site location.
- Concurrence with specific responsibilities.

- Ability to demonstrate how selected business continuity strategies would actually be accomplished.

Planning

Prior feedback summaries, as well as the normal operations and emergency response sections of the contingency plan should be reviewed and specific functions selected for examination.

Examination

Meet with selected users and data processing personnel to determine how well prepared they are to cope with an actual disaster. Examination would include, but not necessarily be limited to, the following considerations:

- Awareness of the plan.
- Accessibility of a copy of the plan at an off-site location.
- Conceptual awareness of specific responsibilities.
- The extent to which the contingency plan has been kept current.
- Strategies for implementing the plan.

Education

Education is an ongoing process during the examination step. It consists of reviewing the intent of the plan, explaining terminology, and recommending various techniques or strategies that might be helpful.

Feedback

Summarize problems and deficiencies and provide specific direction for corrective action.

TECHNOLOGY TESTING

The purpose of testing is to assess specific hardware and/or software capabilities of computers. Testing should be preceded by planning with users and data processing personnel to select a process for testing of the back-up computer processing capability.

Testing should include, but not be limited to:

- Accessibility of backup files at an off-site storage location.
- Retrieval and copying of backup files.
- Establishment of temporary communications lines.
- Limited operation of selected user applications.

Upon completion of testing, feedback provides a documented summary of deficiencies, accompanied by directions for corrective action.

Planning

Meet with data processing personnel to identify specific hardware and/or software capabilities to be tested. Equally important is to sufficiently test alternate telecommunication links to ensure that they can be made operational in the anticipated time frame and that sufficient "load" is simulated to be reasonably confident that the actual demand can be handled during a stabilization period.

Meet with functional department heads to encourage them to participate in testing and to work with them in defining what should be expected from the test. The objective of a true test should not be to see whether the computer runs, but to have the functional business units actually process test data and verify that the results of the test are complete and accurate. It is the business units that should define what constitutes a successful test, not the data processing department. Initially, it is acceptable to notify personnel ahead of time so that they are sufficiently prepared to test; however, as time goes on, it is important to spring some "surprise" tests just to keep people alert and aware that if the real thing happens, this is the way it will be.

Conducting the Test

Testing backup computer processing capability should, as a minimum, provide verification that the proper files and data bases are being stored offsite, that applications can be restored, and that transactions can be properly processed. To accomplish these testing goals at a computer hot-site means actually operating the back-up computer at the hot-site with your own staff. It can be an expensive procedure but a necessary one if redundant processing capability is your strategy. Whatever your solution is, it should be testable. This is a problem with a cold-site strategy.

The basic difficulty with a computer cold-site solution is that it is not practical to test. Cold-site testing would mean having to:

- Have a replacement computer delivered to a cold-site.
- Have the computer installed and made operational.
- Repeat the hot-site testing process previously discussed.
- Return the computer to the vendor and expect the vendor to be able to sell it to someone else as new equipment.

Because a cold-site strategy is for all intents and purposes untestable, it is not a viable solution. The recommended solution is either a computer hot-site or a business continuity plan that stipulates how essential business functions that are normally dependent on computer processing can survive until computer processing capability is restored.

Feedback Summaries

The first suggestion is that a summary of test results can be prepared, not by data processing, but by functional business unit managers. The feedback summary should state the purpose of the test, the specific *measurable* test goals that were established by the business unit managers, the extent to which these goals were achieved, and what corrective action is recommended—including the name of the person responsible for the corrective action and the date by which it should be completed. Previous feedback summaries should be examined at the time a test is planned to ensure that the problem areas remain in order.

9

GUIDELINES FOR INTERNAL CONSULTANTS AND CONSULTING FIRMS

BACKGROUND

Providing quality solutions to client problems is the goal. This emphasis on quality control manifests itself in methods Standards and performance Standards. The objective of these standards is to ensure consistency in data gathering, codification and classification, processing, and report preparation.

Contingency planning, or more specifically, disaster recovery planning constitutes one of the major fields of practice. This specialty is destined to grow in demand and complexity. Much of the growth is the result of increased dependence on computerized systems. The complexity issue is a direct result of the technology explosion.

OBJECTIVES AND SCOPE

Guidelines for Internal Consultants and Consulting Firms was developed to provide methods and performance standards in developing, maintaining, and testing client contingency plans. They have been developed to help consultants control plan development costs while ensuring quality in deliverables. They also contain standards for evaluating consulting staff performance.

Section I recommends organization of the contingency planning function in a client environment. It also emphasizes the importance of senior management's involvement in defining corporate contingency planning policy and strategy.

Section II provides guidelines in project implementation planning. It establishes standards for evaluating client environment, identification of unique requirements, and developing a cost-effective implementation strategy.

Section III covers methods and staff performance standards for developing "what if" business contingency strategies for use during a stabilization period immediately following a disaster. Emphasis is on departmental managers' involvement.

Section IV provides methods and staff performance standards for documenting facility contingency plans. Risk management program documentation format is defined as "procedural"; emergency response plan as "checklist"; and business continuity strategies as "guidelines."

Section V covers institutionalizing plan maintenance and testing. It also covers conducting compliance audits to encourage continued preparedness.

SECTION I: ORGANIZATION

Placement of the Contingency Planning Activity

An increasing dependency on computerized on-line systems and vital facilities underlines the need to place responsibility for data security and disaster recovery responsibilities properly within a company's organization. This is important when one considers that disasters such as fire, explosion, or sabotage can leave facilities inaccessible for several weeks.

It should be emphasized that the real issue in contingency planning is development of practical and workable "what if" business continuity strategies. These strategies accomplish two objectives during a stabilization period immediately following a disaster:

1. Protect market share.
2. Provide continuity in servicing customers.

Development of a disaster recovery plan is really a type of contingency planning or, more correctly, strategic planning. Although the probability of having to activate the plan is extremely remote, there is no doubt it is a strategic planning issue for most companies. It is, therefore, a corporate issue, and responsibility for its success does not belong within the data processing function.

It is recommended that responsibility for contingency plan development and maintenance be positioned in one of the following:

- In manufacturing plant locations, it should be a staff position that reports directly to the plant general manager.
- In corporate headquarters, it should be a staff position that in turn reports to the chief operating officer.

Organizational Functions

A successful contingency planner must be technically competent and have access to all executive management and line management personnel. Moreover, planning, updating existing documentation, staying current with state-of-the-art technology, and supplying reliable information to management involve a high degree of integrity, objectivity, and skill.

A contingency planner should report to one executive and be responsible for the following functions:

- Plan development
- Implementation
- Testing
- Maintenance

Operational effectiveness of a contingency plan is enhanced when sound internal control practices are followed. This is particularly important in developing business continuity strategies for individual departments, in which preparedness depends heavily on familiarity with day-to-day operations.

All persons within the organization should recognize that the disaster recovery planning is important. Accordingly, a major effort should be made to ensure that all individuals responsible for this activity can work effectively with all levels of management. They should have both technical and administrative competence, as well as personality characteristics compatible with those of other key individuals in the organization.

The authority and responsibility for functions that must go on during normal operations should be comprehensively documented. These functions provide the foundation required to support emergency response and the alternate operating practices that will be used during a stabilization period. Precise, written instructions should be prepared and circulated to all key individuals. These day-to-day functions, which are critical to the actual recovery from a disaster, should be institutionalized into daily routines.

Responsibility for specific actions that must be accomplished within hours after an actual disaster occurs also need to be individually cited. In addition, a follow-up mechanism to ensure that they have been completed must be documented. Care must be taken to ensure that these functions will still be performed in spite of personnel loss at the time of a disaster.

"What if" business continuity strategies that will be used to maintain business continuity immediately following a disaster must be clearly documented, including specific guidelines that clarify what alternate methods are expected to be used in lieu of standard procedures. Although "what if" business continuity strategies need not result in detailed procedures, they should be sufficiently explicit that an individual familiar with a particular function can easily visualize how the alternate methods that are expected to be implemented during a stabilization period can be accomplished.

Responsibilities for restoring normal processing capabilities must also be documented so that this function can proceed immediately without delays in approving expenditures. Documentation for communications networks, computer hardware, peripheral equipment, plumbing, air conditioning, and software all need to be readily available from a safe off-site location.

SECTION II: STANDARDS FOR IMPLEMENTATION PLANNING

Methods Standards

Objective. To provide a checklist and guidelines to follow in conducting the strategic planning phase portion of developing a contingency plan.

Review of Environment. Assemble the following information through obtaining copies, interviews, observations, and analysis:

- Organization charts of all departments
- Telephone directory
- Copy of outside auditors and internal auditor comments on disaster recovery needs

Preliminary Statement of Objectives
- Document the following:
  - Objectives of executive management
  - Concerns of key executives
  - Constraints or conditions
- Document exposure to disasters:
  - Tornado
  - Fire
  - Flood
  - Explosion
  - Sabotage
  - Aircraft
  - Work stoppage
  - Y2K
  - Other
- Review any prior attempts to develop a disaster recovery plan:
  - Policy
  - Strategy
  - User participation
  - Procedures:
    Normal operations
    Emergency response
    Stabilization
  - Completeness

- Up-to-date
- Testing
- Preparedness
- Identify vital facilities and critical operations concerned with:
  - Market share
  - Customer service
- Observe operating practices.
- Document hardware configuration.
- Document teleprocessing network.
- Review physical security.
- Review data security.
- Examine vital records program.
- Document the cost of any existing or proposed backup processing sites.
- Review existing backup agreements.
- Develop implementation plan:
  - Tasks
  - Strategy
  - Timetable
  - Effort

Performance Standards

Objective. To provide measurement and reporting techniques to monitor quality and costs.

Elapsed Time
- Elapsed time commitments will be included in proposal letters for each phase of an engagement.
- At the first indication that elapsed time commitments contained in a proposal letter might not be met, it is imperative that a written memo be delivered to the Director of Client Relations within two working days.

- Elapsed time commitments will be subject to review subsequent to the completion of each phase.

Effort
- Man-hours of effort required to complete the following activities are to be reviewed and signature approved by our Director of Client Relations in the "review" copy of the discussion draft proposal:
- Planning
- Meetings (including preparation)
- Data gathering
- Evaluating and organizing
- Business continuity strategies
- Procedure development
- Review and finalize
- Target (budgeted) man-hours (less any man-hours expended in previous months) will be reflected on the current month's time sheet of the project manager.
- Actual hours expended will be recorded against the activity performed on the proper date on each individual's time sheet.
- The project manager will review budgets and hours expended to date weekly and notify Director of Client Relations in memo form of any expected overruns.

SECTION III: STANDARDS FOR DEVELOPING BUSINESS CONTINUITY STRATEGIES

Methods Standards

Objective. To provide a checklist and guidelines to follow in developing business continuity strategies.

Methodology. Development of sound, well-thought-out "what if" business continuity strategies is without question the most important part of developing a successful disaster recovery plan. More importantly, it is an iterative *process* that increasingly calls on your skills to continually do three things well:

1. *Position* your thinking such that you can feel and visualize the concerns of individual users and take the time through multiple get-togethers (as opposed to formal meetings) to listen carefully to their thoughts.
2. *Anticipate* what the problem areas might be, and then formulate conceptually what options might be available as solutions.
3. *Communicate* with other knowledgeable individuals on a casual basis to "check out" the various options and to help you begin to formulate the business continuity strategy you would like endorsed.

In conducting the iterative process, be careful to introduce yourself to the department heads before you meet with first-line supervision. In meetings with the department heads, you should accomplish the following:

- Be professional in your conduct.
- Briefly explain the charter of our engagement.
- Mention our philosophy that contingency planning is a corporate issue and that you fully expect many of the solutions and answers to be developed while working with first-line supervisors.
- Request permission to contact supervisors to get into the details of existing practices and procedures.
- Explain that many times the business continuity strategy that will emerge is a combination of: (1) discontinuing activities that could be done without in a crisis condition; (2) finding alternate methods of obtaining information; or (3) processing data manually until normal processing capability is restored.

It is extremely important to continually strive to drive home the following issues in your discussions with department heads and other users:

- The probability of ever experiencing an actual disaster is extremely remote.
- Communications networking can be the single biggest problem.

- The charter is *not* concerned with brief outages of a few hours or one or two days.
- There is no insurance available that will cover loss of market share, and this is the most critical asset to protect.
- Traditional business functions, such as payroll, invoicing, accounts receivable, and accounts payable, must continue to function.

Performance Standards

Objective. To provide measurement and reporting techniques to monitor quality and costs.

Elapsed Time
- Elapsed time commitments will be included in proposal letters for each phase of an engagement.
- At the first indication that elapsed time commitment might not be met, it is imperative that a written memo be delivered to the director of client relations within two working days.
- Elapsed time commitments will be subject to review subsequent to the completion of each phase.

Effort
- Targeted (budgeted) man-hours (less any man-hours expended in previous months) will be reflected on the current month's time sheet of the project manager for the following activities:
  - Meetings
  - Data gathering
  - Evaluating and organizing
  - Field trips
  - Formulating proposed business continuity strategies
- Actual hours expended will be recorded against the activity performed on the proper date on each individual's time sheet.
- The project manager will review budgets and hours expended to date weekly and notify our Director of Client Relations in memo form of any expected overruns.

SECTION IV: DOCUMENTATION STANDARDS

Methods Standards

Objective. To provide a checklist and guidelines to follow in documenting responsibility for the following time periods:

- Normal processing
- Emergency response
- Stabilizing operations

Methodology. Documentation will be written in the following format:

- Step numbers will be assigned chronologically.
- Responsibilities will be assigned to specific job titles.
- Activity statements must begin with an action verb and be concise.

Risk Management Program. The following activities should be specifically addressed in the risk management program:

- Letter of understanding for use of a backup computer processing site
- Creation of frequency backup copies of:
  - Master files
  - Source programs
  - Data bases
  - Unprocessed transactions
  - Operating system
- Off-site storage of frequently backed-up items
- Creation of latest copies of documentation:
  - Systems documentation
  - Computer operating instructions
- Off-site storage of latest copies of documentation
- Update off-site storage records for current status

- Off-site storage of special forms
- Alternate input methods for future systems
- Develop specifications for current equipment:
  - Air conditioning
  - Electrical
  - Telephones
  - Communications
- Off-site storage of specifications
- Update contingency plan for new systems
- Test preparedness
- Test backup site processing
- Update contingency plan for changes in:
  - Policy and strategy
  - Normal operating procedures
  - Emergency response procedures
  - Business continuity strategies

Emergency Response Plan. The following activities should be specifically addressed in the emergency response plan:

- Activate plan.
- Notify media.
- Notify customers.
- Order replacements for damaged equipment.
- Document historical record of events.
- Provide 24-hour protection at site of disaster.
- Obtain back-up copies of:
  - Frequently backed-up items
  - Documentation
  - Special forms
  - Specifications
- Copy backup items.
- Return backup items to off-site storage.

- Arrange for physical security and data security.
- Supervise packing and moving of files and equipment.
- Arrange for emergency telephone service.
- Establish processing schedules.
- Arrange for expense advances and payment of current expenses.

"What If" Business Continuity Strategies. The following items should be specifically addressed in business continuity strategies:

1. *Loss of data communications*
   - Systems that will continue normal processing (no requirement)
   - Systems that will need minor adjustments in input media to continue normal processing:
     - Specify steps needed to alter input method.
     - Assign specific responsibilities for changing input media.
     - Specify responsibility for accumulating transactions.
     - Specify responsibilities for internal controls.
     - Specify responsibility for updating computer files after normal processing capability has been restored.
     - Specify alternate methods to be used during the stabilization period.
     - Assign responsibility for notifying affected personnel.
     - Assign responsibility for internal controls.
   - Systems that will defer computer processing until after normal processing capability is restored:
     - Specify responsibility for notifying affected personnel.
     - Specify responsibility for accumulating transactions.
     - Specify responsibilities for internal controls.
     - Specify responsibility for updating computer files after normal processing capability has been restored.
   - Functions that will defer computer processing until normal processing capacity is restored and will use alternate methods to support the function:
     - Specify responsibility for notifying affected personnel.

2. *Loss of computer processing capability*
- Systems that will defer computer processing until normal processing capability is restored:
  - Specify responsibility for notifying affected personnel.
  - Specify responsibility for accumulating transactions.
  - Specify responsibility for internal controls.
  - Specify responsibility for updating computer files after normal processing capability has been restored.
  - Specify alternate methods to be used during the interim processing period.
- Systems that will process on a backup computer:
  - Specify responsibility for notifying affected personnel.
  - Specify responsibility for accumulating transactions.
  - Specify responsibility for internal controls
  - Specify responsibility for loading backup files
  - Specify responsibility for contacting: (1) users, (2) production scheduling, (3) computer operators, and (4) application support personnel.
  - Specify responsibility for implementing alternate procedures for obtaining input

3. *Loss of facility access*
- Identify individual business functions.
- Identify administrative and systems support activities that directly impact market share and customer service.
- Develop "what if" business continuity strategies for each support activity and business function.

Performance Standards

Objective. To provide measurement and reporting techniques to monitor quality and costs.

Elapsed Time
- Elapsed time commitments will be included in proposal letters for each phase of an engagement.

- At the first indication that elapsed time commitments might not be met, it is imperative that a written memo be hand delivered to the Director of Client Relations within two working days.
- Elapsed time commitments will be subject to review subsequent to the completion of each phase.

Effort
- Targeted (budgeted) man-hours (less any man-hours expended in previous months) will be reflected on the current month's time sheet of the project manager for the following activities:
  - Meetings
  - Data gathering
  - Evaluating and organizing
  - Field trips
  - Formulating proposed business continuity strategies
- Actual hours expended will be recorded against the activity performed on the proper date on each individual's time sheet.
- The project manager will review budgets and hours expended to date weekly and notify the Director of Client Relations in memo form of any expected overruns.

SECTION V: STANDARDS FOR ONGOING MAINTENANCE AND TESTING

Methods Standards

Objective. To provide a checklist and guidelines to follow in testing interim processing capability and preparedness of personnel to cope with a disaster condition on a timely basis.

Methodology
- Develop a test plan to audit compliance with normal processing procedures for the following activities:
  - Creating backup files
  - Storing backup copies

- Updating documentation
- Updating equipment lists
- Keeping personnel names current
- Updating specifications for current equipment
- Updating manual for new systems
- Document results of the test of preparedness in concise narrative form.
- Develop and document recommendations for improved preparedness.
- Conduct feedback session with affected personnel.
- Conduct follow-up sessions as required.
- Develop a test plan that reveals the awareness of responsible personnel as to their specific responsibilities during the stabilization period and their familiarity with how these responsibilities are to be carried out for such activities as:
  - Activating the plan
  - Notifying personnel
  - Notifying press
  - Notifying customers
  - Ordering replacement equipment
  - Obtaining backup copies
  - Protecting backup copies
  - Arranging for physical security
  - Arranging for emergency telephone service
  - Establishing processing schedules
- Document results of the test in concise narrative form.
- Develop and document recommendations for improved preparedness.
- Conduct feedback sessions.
- Conduct hot-site test and conduct feedback sessions.

Performance Standards

Objectives
- To provide a continuing education process by which preparedness to cope with a disaster situation will be continually improved
- To provide a program to test business continuity strategies

Elapsed Time
- Elapsed time commitments will be included in proposal letters for each phase of an engagement.
- At the first indication that elapsed time commitments might not be met, it is imperative that a written memo be hand delivered to the Director of Client Relations within two working days.
- Elapsed time commitments will be subject to review subsequent to the completion of each phase.

Effort. Targeted (budgeted) man-hours (less any man-hours expended in previous months) will be reflected on the current month's time sheet of the project manager for the following activities:

- Meetings
- Data gathering
- Evaluating and organizing
- Field trips
- Formulating proposed interim processing strategies

APPENDIX A

CASE STUDIES

It was 2:30 on a particularly busy afternoon when Jack McCaffery's phone rang. Jack was vice president of management information systems (MIS) for the Carnegie Tool and Die Company, and at that particular time McCaffery was wishing that he had never gotten involved in computers.

The caller was Dick Strathmeyer, president of Carnegie Tool and Die. "Jack, could you take a few minutes and stop over at my office in a half hour? I've also asked Bill Satterfield and Charlie Jacobs." Satterfield was vice president of operations, and Jacobs was the director of internal audit.

"Sure, I can come," said Jack. "What is the subject to be discussed?"

Strathmeyer explained. "It's our disaster recovery plan. To be honest, I really don't understand what the problem is, but out internal auditors keep saying we don't have a facility contingency plan. I explained to Charlie that you already have put together our computer disaster recovery plan and that we have a hot-site contract with Sundog. But Charlie says that's not enough, that now we need a business continuity plan. Bill claims that over the last 20 years we've spent $11,946,318, mostly on hot-site subscription fees and testing, and that the whole program is a waste of money. As I remember, we originally put our plan together because our outside auditors said we needed a computer disaster recovery plan, and I want to know what our problem is before the auditors get wind of this misunderstanding.

"I need you to explain our contingency program to Bill and Charlie so they feel comfortable."

At 3:15, Jack walked into the president's office. Satterfield was talking, "I've done some checking about this disaster recovery plan and no one in our entire department knows anything about a contingency plan, except that Tom Nelson, who has been here 23 years, has a copy of a questionnaire asking what our critical computer systems were and how long we could operate without them. Beyond that, I know nothing. And besides, the most important issue is not recovering the computer, but determining how we can keep shipping product until conditions return to normal."

Before Jack could say anything, Charlie chimed in. "Bill, we're spending all this money on a backup computer hot-site when I'm not really certain it would actually work or that we even need it at all. I say let's cancel the computer hot-site agreement."

"Wait a minute," said Strathmeyer. "Let's have Jack tell us why we did what we did and what he thinks should be done to get this thing back on track."

"When we started this project," explained Jack, "Dave Myers, who was president before Dick, sent me a memo shortly after our outside auditors criticized us for not having a computer disaster recovery plan. The memo instructed me to develop a computer disaster recovery plan and to have it completed within 90 days. Obviously, there wasn't much time, so we did what we had to in order to meet the deadline. We asked users of our computer system how many days they could do without the computer. The answer came back that after three days our operations would be paralyzed and work would grind to a halt. We concluded that the computer had to be operational within three days, and a backup computer hot-site agreement was the only solution we could find. That's why we have this hot-site agreement that is costing us millions of dollars over several years."

"Hold on a minute, Jack," said Jacobs. "If a disgruntled employee destroyed the entire mainframe computer with a homemade bomb, how many days would it take to get a new computer running?"

"Well," explained Jack, "under normal conditions, it would take about four months to get the requisition approved, place the order, and have the computer installed."

"Stop right there," said Satterfield. "Forget normal conditions!"

"If this thing ever happens, we should be prepared to immediately fax an emergency replacement order within hours—even pick up a used computer temporarily if we have to—and work our computer reps around the clock, authorizing whatever overtime is needed to get back in business quickly. But where would we put a computer while the computer room was being restored?"

"What about the company cafeteria?" asked Strathmeyer. "If we needed to, we could certainly live without a cafeteria for a few weeks or months while the computer room was being repaired. What about it, Jack?"

Jack replied that he never thought about it that way before, but that if he had the authority to immediately order and expedite the delivery of replacement computer equipment and, if needed, could temporarily lease equipment, he felt he could have the computer back up and running in 5 to 10 days, or a maximum of 8 working days.

"Then do we need the backup computer hot-site agreement that's costing us so much money?" asked Strathmeyer.

"Probably not," said Satterfield. "I'll personally guarantee you that if we can expect to have a computer operational, somewhere, somehow, within 5 to 10 days, we will find a way to keep shipping product during that time without any backup computer at all."

After pausing for a moment, Jack said, "Well, if that's the case, then we don't need the hot-site agreement—but we just signed another five-year agreement with Sundog two months ago, so we'll have to wait another five years before we can begin saving the backup computer hot-site subscription fees, to say nothing of the time we've been wasting in maintaining and trying to test our existing plan. I'm certainly glad to have this information—I wish we had known it before we signed the original hot-site agreement. It could actually have saved us millions of dollars."

EPILOGUE

The following four points are key issues:

1. The MIS director should have resisted the ultimatum to have a plan completed within 90 days.
2. Data processing should have established the "window" at 5 to 10 days *before* talking to department heads.
3. The question that should have been asked of department heads was not "How long could you do without?" but "What could you do to keep shipping product for a period of 5 to 10 days until computer processing is restored?"
4. A business continuity plan should have been developed before any thought was given to a data processing plan.

* * * * * * * *

Dave Dean had just been named the new director of information systems at the Keenan Distribution Company and was going through some files that his predecessor, Jim Magin, had left him. One caught his attention. Its title was "Disaster Plan." He began to read. It was very confusing, because it sounded like a series of start–stop, intermittent attempts at a plan that, for some reason, was never completed. Because there were periodic references to audit reports about disaster recovery planning, Dave decided to look at the "Audit Report" folder that was next to the "Disaster Plan" folder in the file. At first he wished he had not looked at it, but then was glad he did, because the problem certainly would not go away, and he might as well face it now.

As he read the latest audit report, he knew it was only a matter of time before Fred Heider, the chief financial officer and his boss, would be on his case. One paragraph in last year's audit report caught his eye. "Once again," he read, "it is our finding that there is no documented disaster recovery plan in the event of a long-term disruption in the accessibility of computer processing capability. Furthermore, the users of these same computer systems have no business continuation plan that documents what their responsibilities will be during a stabilization period.

"It is our recommendation that the highest priority be given to developing a business continuity plan that will at least document guidelines on how users will support essential business functions during a stabilization period.

Dave closed the folder, placed it in his "to do" file, and dialed Jim Andrus. Jim was the quality control manager who had been at Keenan Distribution for 28 years and knew all the company skeletons.

Jim walked into Dave's office and said, "Well, what is it this time?" Dave asked Jim to take a few minutes to tell him what he knew about computer disaster recovery plan development at Keenan.

"It's a mess," said Jim. "We've been working on and off, mostly off, on developing a plan, but something always seems to take a higher priority. We get bogged down in detail, and then the person responsible either gets put on some other project or takes a job with some other company. We've probably been fooling around with this thing for eight years. I remember the first project was headed by Jim Hiering. It took six months, but the only thing that came out of it was a *call list* so out of date it isn't funny, and an obsolete list of computer equipment we had at the time. Then about four years later, there was another flurry following an audit report, and Ann Louise was given the assignment.

"It was decided the first thing we should do is to get our data processing shop protected before we went out and talked to our users about business continuity. We called in our computer vendor to help, but somehow the project got all tangled up in arguing about how many teams we should have. It eventually got stalled, because we decided on 14 different teams and the cost of the disaster recovery program we wanted to purchase would accommodate only four teams. And another thing— finding out what is really critical is almost impossible," said Jim. "Ann sent out a good questionnaire to our users, and you wouldn't believe the answers we got back. On top of that, Ed Kay, our vice president of operations, told us that he didn't want us bothering his managers by taking their time to discuss disaster recovery planning. We had no support from senior management, and the whole thing was unresolved again.

"And then two years ago, it sounded as though we were really going to get the thing done right. We purchased a computer plan development methodology that was supposed to make things easy and straightforward. What a disappointment that turned out to be. The computerized methodology continually dragged us into reams and reams of detail that finally became absurd. We had three of our most experienced analysts, Sarah, Gretchen, and Claire, trying to work with this program. Their desks were piled high with documents and printouts.

"I think they're still in the storage room. The project fell apart when Sarah was transferred to accounting and Gretchen took a job as marketing director of an advertising firm in Boston. As you know, Claire is still here, but she is now running computer operations."

Before Jim could go on, Dave interrupted him. "Thanks for giving me the background, Jim. I think it's time to take a different strategy to put this thing to bed. Give me some time to think it over. Then maybe we can get this plan completed once and for all."

EPILOGUE

This case is not an unfamiliar story. The primary problem has been the lack of a strategy that:

- Focused on business continuity before "getting data processing cleaned up first"
- Contained a proven process for dealing with essential business functions in a concise manner that got the project over with quickly
- Ensured senior management support during plan development.

The solution is to develop a solid project strategy and select a proven plan development methodology. Then sell the strategy and methodology to senior management. This will ensure the support of senior management staff for developing a plan and help them to understand the absolute need to work with functional managers during plan development. The third step is to develop business continuity strategies that support cash flow and servicing customer orders during a stabilization period.

APPENDIX B

SAMPLE COMPUTER CONTINGENCY PLAN

POLICY & STRATEGY

POLICY

The contingency plan policy of the Bestabrand Foods Division is to: (1) ensure an organized and effective response to an isolated disaster that would render telephone communications, remote date communications and/or computer equipment inaccessible or inoperative, or normal work locations inaccessible; and (2) ensure business continuity for business functions dependent on computer technology, until normal processing capability is restored.

STRATEGY

The strategy of the Bestabrand Foods disaster recovery and business continuation plan is as follows:

- Ensure that all relevant computer software and data bases are duplicated and stored in a secure off-site location for use in recovery.

- Provide alternate processing guidelines to support essential business functions and maintain cash flow during a computer disaster recovery period.

- Publish an organized plan that can be used as a reference should a disaster actually occur.

- Identify responsibility to restore voice communications in the event of a loss of telephone service.

- Provide for plan maintenance for environmental and systems changes.

APPENDIX B

EXECUTIVE SUMMARY

The Bestabrand Foods Division disaster recovery and business continuation plan is designed to protect against the sudden loss of telephone communications, data communications and/or computer processing capability through disasters such as fire, water, explosion, aircraft accident, or sabotage. Experience indicates that the probability that such a disaster might occur to a given installation is extremely remote. However, due to present and planned dependency on computer processing, interim processing strategies and guidelines have been developed to protect market share and to ensure that critical business functions can continue to operate until processing capability is restored.

It is expected that computer operations will be able to be restored within eight working days. In a worst case scenario these interim processing strategies could be in effect longer. Although temporary discontinuance of some systems may result in a loss of efficiency, the objective is to prevent a significant deterioration in cash flow and/or the ability to service customers during a disaster recovery period.

Following are the different time periods covered by this plan, along with a summary of contents:

NORMAL OPERATIONS

This phase of the program addresses normal operating practices that should be followed to minimize the impact of a localized disaster and to provide the foundation for an organized response and ensure business continuity during a disaster recovery period. It assigns direct responsibility for specific actions, including periodic testing of user interim processing capability.

EMERGENCY RESPONSE

Responsibility to alert senior management of the need to activate this plan rests with the information systems manager or his designate.

The specifics of a recovery program can only be determined at the time a disaster occurs. This depends on the nature of the disaster, the point in time that the disaster occurs, and the anticipated period of disruption. Plan activation requires global knowledge of management information systems and control of systems support resources.

The emergency response section identifies activities that will need attention immediately following an incident/disaster. It is intended to ensure an organized response and to provide a checklist of issues that need attention.

152

APPENDIX B

INTERIM PROCESSING

The interim processing period represents the time during which interim processing strategies will be used to protect market share and provide support to essential business functions. These interim processing strategies and guidelines have been developed by operating personnel who are the ones most knowledgeable concerning their needs and capability to service customers during a disaster recovery period.

RESTORATION

Restoration is the process of executing plans for reconstruction of a computer center and restoration of normal computer processing. This will include finalizing drawings, obtaining and executing contractor bids, ordering and installing computer hardware and telecommunications equipment, and obtaining furniture and supplies.

APPENDIX B

MAINTENANCE AND USER CONTINUING EDUCATION AND PREPAREDNESS REVIEWS

Because disaster recovery and business continuation plans are environmentally dependent, effective maintenance, user continuing education and preparedness reviews, and backup computer testing programs are needed. Their purpose is to:

- Assure viability of user interim processing strategies through a program of continuing education and preparedness evaluation.

- Update and maintain contingency plans for systems changes, hardware upgrades, and assigned responsibilities.

- Test backup computer processing capability.

MAINTENANCE

Systems changes and additions should be reviewed quarterly to ensure that new customer services or modifications to existing services have not invalidated existing interim processing strategies. These interim processing strategies should be reviewed with data processing to make certain that computer processing plans are compatible with these strategies.

Reviews should also be conducted to ensure awareness of data processing responsibilities during normal operations, emergency response, and restoration time periods.

NORMAL OPERATIONS

Activities in the normal operations section form the foundation upon which much of the plan is based. There is a great deal of dependency on this section. Annual reviews should be scheduled to examine and update these procedures /personnel assignments to prevent the plan from deteriorating and becoming obsolete.

EMERGENCY RESPONSE

Meetings should be scheduled annually with selected users, systems analysts, and data processing personnel to ensure that promotions and attrition have not affected assigned responsibilities.

RESTORATION

Restoration activities are impacted by all environmental changes, including modifications to other segments of the plan. Restoration plans should be reviewed annually to ensure that these changes and modifications have been considered in the restoration of normal processing.

APPENDIX B

INTERIM PROCESSING STRATEGIES

Interim processing strategies should be reviewed annually with user departments to ensure that new customer services or modifications to existing services have not invalidated interim processing strategies. The interim processing strategies should in turn be reviewed with data processing to make certain that computer processing continues to be compatible with capacities and capabilities.

USER CONTINUING EDUCATION AND PREPAREDNESS REVIEWS

In order to ensure that a plan is workable, users need to be aware of their responsibilities and be prepared to implement them in the event of a disaster. Through a continuing program of education, periodic preparedness review, and evaluation, user awareness can be maintained.

On a selected basis, users should be examined to determine how well prepared they are to cope with an actual disaster. The examination should include, but not necessarily be limited to, the following considerations:

- Awareness of the plan.

- Accessibility to a copy of the plan from an off-site location.

- Concurrence with specific responsibilities.

- Ability to demonstrate how selected interim processing strategies would actually be accomplished.

PLANNING

Prior feedback summaries as well as the normal operations, emergency response, and restoration sections of the disaster recovery plan should be reviewed and specific functions selected for examination.

EXAMINATION

Meet with selected users and data processing personnel to determine how well prepared they are to cope with an actual disaster. Examination would include, but not necessarily be limited to, the following considerations:

155

APPENDIX B

- Awareness of the plan.

- Accessibility to a copy of the plan from an off-site location.

- Conceptual awareness of specific responsibilities.

- The extent to which the disaster recovery plan has been kept current.

- Strategies for implementing the plan.

EDUCATION

Education is an ongoing process during the examination step. It consists of reviewing intent of the plan, explaining terminology, and recommending various techniques or strategies that might be helpful.

FEEDBACK

Summarize problems and deficiencies accompanied by specific direction for correction action.

APPENDIX B

NORMAL OPERATIONS

Normal operations outlines tasks and responsibilities
necessary to support and maintain an effective ongoing
disaster recovery and business continuation plan, before a
localized disaster occurs.

Responsibility	Action
1. Operations manager	Ensure that all relevant files and data bases are consistently backed up in accordance with the processing frequency indicated on application data sheets.
2. Senior operator	Rotate magnetic tapes representing data base and data sets based on existing daily, weekly, and monthly schedules to the off-site location.
3. Operations manager	Store source programs, compiled programs, operating systems, data communication , and related system software at the off-site location.
4. Operations manager	Maintain up-to-date documentation to support production scheduling and computer operations, at the off-site location.
5. Operations manager	Maintain current applications data entry procedures and program documentation at the off-site location.
6. Operations manager	Maintain specifications for the following items: a. Air conditioning (make/model) b. Electrical (outlets/power requirements/room layout) c. Central processors (make/model) d. Peripheral equipment (make/model) e. Telecommunications (vendor/make/model) f. Telephones (vendor/make/model)

APPENDIX B

7. Operations manager   Store specifications at the off-site location.

8. Operations manager   Arrange for annual review of interim processing strategies and guidelines.

9. Applications manager   Ensure that future systems and/or software acquisitions are integrated into the plan.

10. Operations manager   Retain copy of the contingency plan at the off-site location.

11. Information systems manager   Arrange for annual review of the normal operations, emergency response, and data center restoration sections of this manual.

12. Operations manager   Review, test, and modify physical security systems and procedures as required, annually.

13. Operations manager   Annually review, test, and modify data security systems and procedures as required.

14. Operations manager   Conduct periodic selective tests of specific Users groups ability to sustain critical business functions by other means, until normal processing capability is restored.

15. Operations manager   Annually update a list of all employees with private cellular telephones.

16. Operations manager   Annually document two sources of replacement hardware.

17. Operations manager   Have on deposit at the off-site storage facility those supplies required to initially support computer operations.

APPENDIX B

NORMAL OPERATIONS (Cont.)

18. Operations manager   Ensure that the following special forms can be obtained from form vendors within one week, or are stored at the off-site location:

        Payroll checks   Payable checks
        Customer order   Invoice
        Statement   Loading order
        Contract

19. Operations manager   Annually update all documents contained in the Appendix.
20. Operations manager   Print Tape Management Catalog monthly and store in off-site location.
21. Operations manager   Ensure that copies of any contractual agreements concerning data center restoration are stored at the off-site location.
22. Operations manager   Annually update employees with cellular phones list (Appendix) in the event normal phone service is disrupted.
23. Operations manager   Annually update minimum office requirements list (Appendix) in the event normal work locations become unacessible.
24. Operations manager   Annually update emergency response notification list (Appendix).
25. Operations manager   Annually update restoration priority list (Appendix).
26. Operations manager   Annually update the name and phone number of the individual to contact to install emergency phone service:

        Name:

        Phone:

APPENDIX B

EMERGENCY RESPONSE

Emergency response identifies required tasks and responsibilities that: (1) must be addressed at the time a specific disaster occurs; or (2) are needed to establish temporary data processing capability at another location. It contains actions assigned to specific individuals as well as an emergency response team that may perform individually or collectively during the emergency response period, at the discretion of the information systems manager.

	Responsibility	Action
1.	Information systems manager	Determine whether the disaster recovery and business continuation plan will be activated. Notify appropriate personnel (see Appendix).
2.	Operations manager	Initiate any reconstruction that might be required at a temporary data processing location.
3.	Operations manager	Document a chronological list of all key events surrounding the disaster emergency response actions and interim processing activities.
4.	Operations manager	Instruct user department managers to execute plans for implementing interim processing strategies and guidelines.
5.	Operations manager	Notify proper authorities, such as police and fire department, based on the nature of the disaster.
6.	Operations manager	Expedite installation of new telephone/communications systems as required.
7.	Information systems manager	Coordinate efforts between the computer and User communities until normal processing capability is restored.
8.	Information systems manager	Survey damage and prepare reconstruction plan for data center.

APPENDIX B

9. Corporate communications manager — Notify media immediately and remain in contact throughout the interim processing period.

10. Operations manager — Survey communications damage and arrange for installation of temporary phone service, as needed.

11. Building services — Establish physical security.

12. Information systems manager — Identify the address and phone number of a temporary network control center (if needed based on the nature of the disaster).

13. Network systems support — Install data communications lines at temporary data processing locations, as directed by the information systems manager.

14. Operations manager — In the absence of any other information, it is recommended that systems be restored in the sequence indicated on the restoration priority list (Index).

15. Operations manager — Refer to employees with cellular phones (Appendix) and contact as necessary to assist in restoring temporary phone services.

16. Information systems manager — Contact personnel on the emergency response notification list (Appendix), as appropriate.

17. Information systems manager — Refer to Minimum Office Requirements (Appendix) in the event it is necessary to set up temporary work locations.

18. Information systems manager — Coordinate shipment and installation of replacement hardware and peripheral equipment.

19. Operations manager — Contact vendors and place emergency replacement orders for replacement equipment. Authorize overtime.

APPENDIX B

EMERGENCY RESPONSE (Cont.)

20. Operations manager   Identify at which site
replacement computer equipment
will be installed (if the normal
site is not available).
Immediately place emergency work
orders to have the site prepared.
Authorize overtime.

21. Operations manager   Refer to Normal Operations #26 in
the event it is necessary to
install emergency phone service.

APPENDIX B

System name: **ACCOUNTS PAYABLE**

System description:

This system facilitates vouchering of approved invoices and check processing. The system also permits on-line generation of checks for COD deliveries.

Key reports:

Checks
Check register
Transaction log

On-line inquiry capability:

Invoice status

Applications dependent on output from this system:

General ledger

APPENDIX B

System name: **ACCOUNTS PAYABLE**

Interim processing guidelines highlight activities to be addressed in support of interim processing strategies. Following are the interim processing guidelines for this system:

A. Startup

   The following steps should be taken in anticipation of implementing interim processing guidelines:

   •   Instruct plant and mill locations to pay grain invoices manually.

B. Interim processing

   Following are processing guidelines that will be in effect until normal computer processing is restored:

   •   Accounts payable pay selected vendor invoices manually to maximize discount allowances.

   •   Trader offices prepare vendor checks manually.

C. Restoration of computerized data

   Records of the following business transactions should be retained so that data files can be updated when normal computer processing is restored:

   •   Manual checks

APPENDIX B

System name: **ACCOUNTS RECEIVABLE**

System description:

This system provides timely planning information to manage cash flow, minimize bad debt loss, and analyze customer activity. It includes invoice posting and on-line cash application. The system is linked directly to the general ledger system.

Key reports:

Aging
Cash application
Receipts

On-line inquiry capability:

Customer account balance

Applications dependent on output from this system:

General ledger
Electronic data interchange (EDI)

APPENDIX B

INTERIM PROCESSING GUIDELINES

System name: **ACCOUNTS RECEIVABLE**

Interim processing guidelines highlight activities to be addressed in support of interim processing strategies. Following are the interim processing guidelines for this system:

A. Startup

The following steps should be taken in anticipation of implementing interim processing guidelines:

- Notify credit that cash application will be deferred until normal computer processing capability is restored.

B. Interim processing

Following are processing guidelines that will be in effect until normal computer processing is restored:

- Deposit checks.

- Defer cash application until normal computer processing capability is restored.

C. Restoration of computerized data

Records of the following business transactions should be retained so that data files can be updated when normal computer processing is restored:

- Cash receipts

- Cash application

APPENDIX B

System name: **BAKERY MIX** _____

System description:

This system contains raw material specifications, yields, and quantities required to produce customer demands. The mills use this information to plan production and to help determine order quantities for raw materials.

Key reports:

Inventory
Six-week explosion
Raw material consumption (RMC)
Usage and adjustment

On-line inquiry capability:

Inventory status

Applications dependent on output from this system:

Flour product specifications

APPENDIX B

<u>INTERIM PROCESSING GUIDELINES</u>

System name: **BAKERY MIX**

Interim processing guidelines highlight activities to be addressed in support of interim processing strategies. Following are the interim processing guidelines for this system:

A. Startup

   The following steps should be taken in anticipation of implementing interim processing guidelines:

   • Obtain copy of latest inventory status report.

B. Interim processing

   Following are processing guidelines that will be in effect until normal computer processing is restored:

   • Use prior orders to help calculate raw material requirements and schedule production manually until normal computer processing capability is restored.

   • Use personal computer (PC) spreadsheet to document inventory transactions.

   • Update inventory status report manually.

C. Restoration of computerized data

   Records of the following business transactions should be retained so that data files can be updated when normal computer processing is restored:

   • Receipts

   • Usage

   • Purchase orders

   • Material transfers

APPENDIX B

System name: **CAR TRACING**

System description:

This system is used to maximize the utilization of
railroad cars. It utilizes car movement information from
carrier databases to update status and location.

Key reports:

None

On-line inquiry capability:

Bill of lading
Car location

Applications dependent on output from this system:

None

APPENDIX B

System name: **CAR TRACING**

Interim processing guidelines highlight activities to be addressed in support of interim processing strategies. Following are the interim processing guidelines for this system:

A. Startup

    The following steps should be taken in anticipation of implementing interim processing guidelines:

    •   Notify plants that TRACE II reports will not be prepared until normal computer processing capability is restored.

B. Interim processing

    Following are processing guidelines that will be in effect until normal computer processing is restored:

    •   Contact carriers to obtain car status and location information.

C. Restoration of computerized data

    Records of the following business transactions should be retained so that data files can be updated when normal computer processing is restored:

    •   Execute TRACE II

APPENDIX B

System name: **CUSTOM FARM PRODUCTS POINT OF SALE**

System description:

This system uses laptop computers containing critical product and customer information to facilitate customized feed formulations. Firm orders are subsequently data entered from field office locations.

Key reports:

Customer orders
Sales inquiries

On-line inquiry capability:

Customer information
Inventory status
Order history

Applications dependent on output from this system:

General ledger

APPENDIX B

System name: **CUSTOM FARM PRODUCTS POINT OF SALE**

Interim processing guidelines highlight activities to be addressed in support of interim processing strategies. Following are the interim processing guidelines for this system:

A. Startup

   The following steps should be taken in anticipation of implementing interim processing guidelines:

   - If outage occurs during the closing cycle, instruct field locations to fax: invoice journals and payment journals.

B. Interim processing

   Following are processing guidelines that will be in effect until normal computer processing is restored:

   - Field offices prepare customer orders manually.

   - Field offices administer orders manually.

   - Field offices prepare invoices manually.

   - Field offices generate month-end reports manually.

C. Restoration of computerized data

   Records of the following business transactions should be retained so that data files can be updated when normal computer processing is restored:

   - Customer orders

   - Invoices

APPENDIX B

System name: **DELIVERY/SALES ANALYSIS**

System description:

This system generates sales reports reflecting revenue as well as material and production costs. These reports are segmented by sales region and territory.

Key reports:

Sales/marketing analysis
Delivery analysis

On-line inquiry capability:

None

Applications dependent on output from this system:

None

APPENDIX B

System name: **DELIVERY/SALES ANALYSIS**

Interim processing guidelines highlight activities to be addressed in support of interim processing strategies. Following are the interim processing guidelines for this system:

A. Startup

The following steps should be taken in anticipation of implementing interim processing guidelines:

- Notify marketing that delivery/sales analysis reports will be prepared after normal computer processing capability is restored.

B. Interim processing

Following are processing guidelines that will be in effect until normal computer processing is restored:

- None

C. Restoration of computerized data

Records of the following business transactions should be retained so that data files can be updated when normal computer processing is restored:

- None

174

APPENDIX B

System name: **ELECTRONIC DATA INTERCHANGE (EDI)**

System description:

This system allows application systems to interact with trading partners electronically for transactions such as orders, shipments, invoices, and payments.

The system also facilitates the direct transfer of funds electronically. It can be used to receive payments from customers or to pay invoices or freight bills.

Key reports:

None

On-line inquiry capability:

None

Applications dependent on output from this system:

Accounts payable
Accounts receivable
Flour order processing
Transportation rates and routes

APPENDIX B

<u>INTERIM PROCESSING GUIDELINES</u>

System name: **ELECTRONIC DATA INTERCHANGE (EDI)**

Interim processing guidelines highlight activities to be addressed in support of interim processing strategies. Following are the interim processing guidelines for this system:

A. Startup

   The following steps should be taken in anticipation of implementing interim processing guidelines:

   • Notify customers, vendors, and Pillsbury personnel to use either phone, fax, or mail to communicate messages until normal computer processing capability is restored.

B. Interim processing

   Following are processing guidelines that will be in effect until normal computer processing is restored:

   • None

C. Restoration of computerized data

   Records of the following business transactions should be retained so that data files can be updated when normal computer processing is restored:

   • Notify customers, vendors, and Pillsbury personnel that EDI is operational.

APPENDIX B

System name: **FLOUR CONTRACTS**

System description:

This system reflects the status of customer agreements to purchase specific amounts of flour at a given price. It reflects prices, delivery time periods, volumes for each customer, shipments-to-date, and unshipped balances.

Key reports:

Flour contracts

On-line inquiry capability:

None

Applications dependent on output from this system:

Order processing
Invoicing

APPENDIX B

System name: **FLOUR CONTRACTS**

Interim processing guidelines highlight activities to be addressed in support of interim processing strategies. Following are the interim processing guidelines for this system:

A. Startup

The following steps should be taken in anticipation of implementing interim processing guidelines:

- Obtain latest copy of price list.

B. Interim processing

Following are processing guidelines that will be in effect until normal computer processing is restored:

- Prepare flour contracts manually.

- Post shipment information to flour contracts manually.

C. Restoration of computerized data

Records of the following business transactions should be retained so that data files can be updated when normal computer processing is restored:

- Flour contracts

- Shipments

APPENDIX B

SYSTEM PROFILE

System name: **FLOUR INVENTORY**

System description:

    This system maintains current inventory levels for
Bestabrand System products. Inventories are costed and
status reports generated daily. Inventory transactions
are transmitted to the HQIC inventory control system.

Key reports:

    Stock status

On-line inquiry capability:

    None

Applications dependent on output from this system:

    None

APPENDIX B

System name: **FLOUR INVENTORY**

Interim processing guidelines highlight activities to be addressed in support of interim processing strategies. Following are the interim processing guidelines for this system:

A. Startup

   The following steps should be taken in anticipation of implementing interim processing guidelines:

   - Obtain latest copy of stock status report.

B. Interim processing

   Following are processing guidelines that will be in effect until normal computer processing is restored:

   - Manually update stock status for raw material receipts based on vendor invoices and receiving reports.

   - Update stock status for usage manually from notices of shipment.

   - Value inventory at last transaction value.

C. Restoration of computerized data

   Records of the following business transactions should be retained so that data files can be updated when normal computer processing is restored:

   - Inventory transfers

APPENDIX B

System name: **FLOUR INVOICING**

System description:

This system receives notices of shipments electronically from shipping locations. It calculates freight, prices products, updates inventory balances, computes extra charges, and prints invoices.

Key reports:

Invoices
Invoice register
On order/held

On-line inquiry capability:

Customer history
Freight rates
Product pricing

Applications dependent on output from this system:

Accounts receivable
Delivery/sales analysis
Flour inventory
General ledger

APPENDIX B .

System name: **FLOUR INVOICING**

Interim processing guidelines highlight activities to be
addressed in support of interim processing strategies.
Following are the interim processing guidelines for this
system:

A. Startup

   The following steps should be taken in anticipation of
   implementing interim processing guidelines:

   • Obtain latest copies of customer list, price list,
     and freight rates.

B. Interim processing

   Following are processing guidelines that will be in
   effect until normal computer processing is restored:

   • Prepare invoices manually until normal computer
     processing capability is restored.

C. Restoration of computerized data

   Records of the following business transactions should be
   retained so that data files can be updated when normal
   computer processing is restored:

   • Manual invoices

APPENDIX B

System name: **FLOUR ORDER PROCESSING**

System description:

This system processes orders for flour milling, food service, and bakery mix. Orders are acknowledged and loading orders printed based on production schedules. The system references a data base of customer information reflecting prior order history, product specifications, special processing instructions, and the names of key personnel.

Key reports:

Loading orders
Order register

On-line inquiry capability:

None

Applications dependent on output from this system:

Flour contracts
Flour inventory
Flour production and shipments

183

APPENDIX B

System name: **FLOUR ORDER PROCESSING**

Interim processing guidelines highlight activities to be addressed in support of interim processing strategies. Following are the interim processing guidelines for this system:

A. Startup

The following steps should be taken in anticipation of implementing interim processing guidelines:

- Obtain copy of outstanding customer orders.

B. Interim processing

Following are processing guidelines that will be in effect until normal computer processing is restored:

- Fax loading orders to plants/mills.

- Fax notice of shipments to order processing.

- Update status of customer orders manually.

C. Restoration of computerized data

Records of the following business transactions should be retained so that data files can be updated when normal computer processing is restored:

- New orders

- Loading orders

- Notices of shipment

APPENDIX B

System name: **FLOUR PRICING** _____

System description:

This system maintains the pricing structure for products including price differentials and promotions.

Key reports:

Pricing differentials

On-line inquiry capability:

Product pricing

Applications dependent on output from this system:

None

APPENDIX B

INTERIM PROCESSING GUIDELINES

System name: **FLOUR PRICING**

Interim processing guidelines highlight activities to be addressed in support of interim processing strategies. Following are the interim processing guidelines for this system:

A. Startup

The following steps should be taken in anticipation of implementing interim processing guidelines:

- Obtain latest price list.

B. Interim processing

Following are processing guidelines that will be in effect until normal computer processing is restored:

- Note price changes on price list.

- Notify sales and marketing of any price changes.

C. Restoration of computerized data

Records of the following business transactions should be retained so that data files can be updated when normal computer processing is restored:

- Price changes

APPENDIX B

System name: **FLOUR PRODUCT SPECIFICATIONS**

System description:

This system maintains technical product specifications, recipes, standard costs, production processes, food safety requirements and quality assurance standards.

Key reports:

None

On-line inquiry capability:

None

Applications dependent on output from this system:

Bakery mix

APPENDIX B

<u>INTERIM PROCESSING GUIDELINES</u>

System name: **FLOUR PRODUCT SPECIFICATIONS**

Interim processing guidelines highlight activities to be addressed in support of interim processing strategies. Following are the interim processing guidelines for this system:

A. Startup

   The following steps should be taken in anticipation of implementing interim processing guidelines:

   • None

B. Interim processing

   Following are processing guidelines that will be in effect until normal computer processing is restored:

   • Accumulate file maintenance transactions until normal computer processing capability is restored.

C. Restoration of computerized data

   Records of the following business transactions should be retained so that data files can be updated when normal computer processing is restored:

   • Product specification changes

   • Recipe changes

   • Quality control standards changes

   • Cost standards changes

SYSTEM PROFILE

System name: **FLOUR PRODUCTION AND SHIPMENTS**

System description:

   This system assimilates reported production daily,
   effects transfer of inventories between raw material and
   finished goods, and tags shipments for invoicing.

Key reports:

   Production control

On-line inquiry capability:

   Inventory status

Applications dependent on output from this system:

   Delivery/sales analysis
   Flour invoicing

APPENDIX B

<u>INTERIM PROCESSING GUIDELINES</u>

System name: **FLOUR PRODUCTION AND SHIPMENTS**

Interim processing guidelines highlight activities to be addressed in support of interim processing strategies. Following are the interim processing guidelines for this system:

A. Startup

The following steps should be taken in anticipation of implementing interim processing guidelines:

- None

B. Interim processing

Following are processing guidelines that will be in effect until normal computer processing is restored:

- Prepare customer orders manually and fax to plants.

- Post production to copy of customer order.

- Fax notice of shipments to customer service for invoicing.

C. Restoration of computerized data

Records of the following business transactions should be retained so that data files can be updated when normal computer processing is restored:

- Production

- Notices of shipment

APPENDIX B

System name: **FREIGHT BILL AUDIT**

System description:

    This system electronically audits freight bills by comparing bill of lading and freight rate information to actual freight bills.

Key reports:

    Audit rejects

On-line inquiry capability:

    Bill of lading
    Freight bill

Applications dependent on output from this system:

    Accounts payable
    General ledger

APPENDIX B

System name: **FREIGHT BILL AUDIT**

Interim processing guidelines highlight activities to be
addressed in support of interim processing strategies.
Following are the interim processing guidelines for this
system:

A. Startup

    The following steps should be taken in anticipation of
    implementing interim processing guidelines:

    •   Create manual control log of unaudited freight
        bills sent to accounts payable.

B. Interim processing

    Following are processing guidelines that will be in
    effect until normal computer processing is restored:

    •   Release unaudited freight bills for payment.

    •   Xerox copies of unaudited freight bills.

    •   Post unaudited freight bills to control log.

C. Restoration of computerized data

    Records of the following business transactions should be
    retained so that data files can be updated when normal
    computer processing is restored:

    •   Unaudited freight bills

APPENDIX B

System name: **GENERAL LEDGER**

System description:

This system provides easy and controlled entry of journal data, automatic data processing, extensive audit trail and management reporting, allocations capability and budgeting. It receives data directly from accounts payable, accounts receivable, payroll, and fixed assets.

Key reports:

Trial balance
Profit and loss statement

On-line inquiry capability:

Chart of account balances

Applications dependent on output from this system:

None

APPENDIX B

System name: **GENERAL LEDGER**

Interim processing guidelines highlight activities to be addressed in support of interim processing strategies. Following are the interim processing guidelines for this system:

A. Startup

   The following steps should be taken in anticipation of implementing interim processing guidelines:

   •   Obtain copies of statements for current month/last year, and prior month/current year.

B. Interim processing

   Following are processing guidelines that will be in effect until normal computer processing is restored:

   •   If outage occurs during the month-end closing cycle, use top-line estimates to close books.

C. Restoration of computerized data

   Records of the following business transactions should be retained so that data files can be updated when normal computer processing is restored:

   •   Estimated journal entries

APPENDIX B

System name: **GRAIN CONTRACTS**

System description:

This on-line system reflects the net cash position of various commodities in which Pillsbury has purchase and sales contracts. Future prices are obtained electronically from the Grain Exchange, and cash prices are data entered manually.

Key reports:

Grain supplies and position
Bulk raw material prices

On-line inquiry capability:

Flour inventory

Applications dependent on output from this system:

None

APPENDIX B

<u>INTERIM PROCESSING GUIDELINES</u>

System name: **GRAIN CONTRACTS**

Interim processing guidelines highlight activities to be addressed in support of interim processing strategies. Following are the interim processing guidelines for this system:

A. Startup

The following steps should be taken in anticipation of implementing interim processing guidelines:

- Obtain latest copy of Daily Grain Supplies and Position and Daily Hedging reports.

B. Interim processing

Following are processing guidelines that will be in effect until normal computer processing is restored:

- Prepare grain contracts manually.

- Update Daily Grain Supplies and Position and Daily Hedging reports manually, based on daily transactions.

C. Restoration of computerized data

Records of the following business transactions should be retained so that data files can be updated when normal computer processing is restored:

- New contracts

- Futures transactions

APPENDIX B

System name: **MAINTENANCE**

System description:

This system generates work orders for mill preventive
maintenance and provides a history of breakdowns for each
piece of capital equipment. This information is used to
plan future maintenance work and in cost analysis for
equipment replacement decisions.

Key reports:

Crew schedules
Parts inventory
Work orders

On-line inquiry capability:

Capital equipment
Component failure

Applications dependent on output from this system:

Accounts payable

APPENDIX B

System name: **MAINTENANCE**

Interim processing guidelines highlight activities to be addressed in support of interim processing strategies. Following are the interim processing guidelines for this system:

A. Startup

The following steps should be taken in anticipation of implementing interim processing guidelines:

- Obtain latest copy of crew schedule.

B. Interim processing

Following are processing guidelines that will be in effect until normal computer processing is restored:

- Schedule preventive maintenance from existing crew schedule.

- Schedule emergency repair work manually.

- Defer scheduling additional preventive maintenance until normal computer processing capability is restored.

C. Restoration of computerized data

Records of the following business transactions should be retained so that data files can be updated when normal computer processing is restored:

- Completed work orders

APPENDIX B

SYSTEM PROFILE

System name: **MASTER PRODUCTION SCHEDULE**

System description:

  This system contains the production load for all
  production facilities. It is updated daily for new
  requirements, shipments and changes. Reports are used to
  schedule production and personnel.

Key reports:

  Flour production
  Bin inventories

On-line inquiry capability:

  Production status
  Production schedule

Applications dependent on output from this system:

  Flour order processing
  Flour production and shipments
  Grain contracts

APPENDIX B

System name: **MASTER PRODUCTION SCHEDULE**

Interim processing guidelines highlight activities to be
addressed in support of interim processing strategies.
Following are the interim processing guidelines for this
system:

A. Startup

The following steps should be taken in anticipation of
implementing interim processing guidelines:

- Obtain latest copy of master production schedule.

B. Interim processing

Following are processing guidelines that will be in
effect until normal computer processing is restored:

- Update latest copy of master production schedule
manually until normal computer processing
capability is restored.

- Communicate any changes in production requirements
to mills.

C. Restoration of computerized data

Records of the following business transactions should be
retained so that data files can be updated when normal
computer processing is restored:

- Production schedule changes

APPENDIX B

System name: **OFFICE AUTOMATION**

System description:

This system supports electronic mail, word processing, time management, file servers, and print servers.

Key reports:

None

On-line inquiry capability:

None

Applications dependent on output from this system:

None

APPENDIX B

<u>INTERIM PROCESSING GUIDELINES</u>

System name: **OFFICE AUTOMATION**

Interim processing guidelines highlight activities to be
addressed in support of interim processing strategies.
Following are the interim processing guidelines for this
system:

A. Startup

The following steps should be taken in anticipation of
implementing interim processing guidelines:

- Notify all users that they should use alternate
methods until normal computer processing capability
is restored.

B. Interim processing

Following are processing guidelines that will be in
effect until normal computer processing is restored:

ELECTRONIC MAIL

- Instruct users to use fax, phones, interoffice
mail, or courier service for messaging.

WORD PROCESSING

- For one-time usage, recommend local word processing
services or the acquisition of a PC-based word
processing package.

- For data base requirements, retrieve backup tapes
and utilize another Pillsbury facility.

TIME MANAGEMENT

- Update latest copy of calendar manually until
normal computer processing capability is restored.

FILE SERVERS

- Download files to PC for local processing.

PRINT SERVERS

- Recable from network printer direct to PC printer.

C. Restoration of computerized data

Records of the following business transactions should be
retained so that data files can be updated when normal
computer processing is restored:

- Notify users that office automation is operational.

APPENDIX B

System name: **SCD INVOICING**

System description:

This system is used by traders to generate customer
invoices' based on commodity shipments. It calculates
freight, prices products, updates inventory balances,
computes extra charges, and prints invoices.

Key reports:

Aged accounts receivable
Invoices
Sales register

On-line inquiry capability:

Order status

Applications dependent on output from this system:

Accounts receivable

APPENDIX B

System name: **SCD INVOICING**

Interim processing guidelines highlight activities to be addressed in support of interim processing strategies. Following are the interim processing guidelines for this system:

A. Startup

   The following steps should be taken in anticipation of implementing interim processing guidelines:

   • Traders prepare list of "credit sensitive" customers for which outstanding balances need to be updated manually on a daily basis.

B. Interim processing

   Following are processing guidelines that will be in effect until normal computer processing is restored:

   • Manually update outstanding balances for "credit sensitive" customers daily.

   • Traders prepare customer invoices manually.

C. Restoration of computerized data

   Records of the following business transactions should be retained so that data files can be updated when normal computer processing is restored:

   • Manual invoices

   • Cash application

APPENDIX B

System name: **TRADER WORKSTATION**

System description:

This system permits traders to share common up-to-date information on special commodities. It allows traders to track contract commitments from purchase origin to sales destination. Other data is obtained directly from news services, commodity exchanges and freight tariffs. The system also provides control accounts for positions and profit information, which summarize daily commodity transactions. It does not tie transactions to specific purchase obligations or delivery commitments, but continually updates long or short positions.

Key reports:

Position
Daily trading activity

On-line inquiry capability:

Contracts
Customer profile
Inventory status
Position
Shipments

Applications dependent on output from this system:

General ledger

APPENDIX B

<u>INTERIM PROCESSING GUIDELINES</u>

System name: **TRADER WORKSTATION**

Interim processing guidelines highlight activities to be addressed in support of interim processing strategies. Following are the interim processing guidelines for this system:

A. Startup

The following steps should be taken in anticipation of implementing interim processing guidelines:

- Obtain latest copy of lineup sheet.

- Obtain latest position report.

- Obtain copies of all active sales and purchase contracts

- Obtain copy of Canadian currency contracts.

B. Interim processing

Following are processing guidelines that will be in effect until normal computer processing is restored:

- Contact other traders to determine marketplace activity.

- Prepare commodity contracts manually.

- Update lineup sheets manually.

C. Restoration of computerized data

Records of the following business transactions should be retained so that data files can be updated when normal computer processing is restored:

- Contracts

- Shipments

- Inventory adjustments

APPENDIX B

System name: **TRANSPORTATION RATES & ROUTES**

System description:

This system maintains a data base of critical
transportation information, such as contract and tariff
rates, routes, and restrictions and limitations, by
carrier.

Key reports:

None

On-line inquiry capability:

Routes
Rates
Least-cost routes

Applications dependent on output from this system:

None

APPENDIX B

System name: **TRANSPORTATION RATES & ROUTES**

Interim processing guidelines highlight activities to be addressed in support of interim processing strategies. Following are the interim processing guidelines for this system:

A. Startup

The following steps should be taken in anticipation of implementing interim processing guidelines:

- Obtain latest copy of published tariffs and railroad contracts.

B. Interim processing

Following are processing guidelines that will be in effect until normal computer processing is restored:

- Assign more experienced personnel to verify routes and rates for repetitive type shipments.

- Refer to published tariffs and/or railroad contracts for less repetitive shipments.

C. Restoration of computerized data

Records of the following business transactions should be retained so that data files can be updated when normal computer processing is restored:

- Tariff changes

- Railroad contract changes

APPENDIX B

RESTORATION

Restoration involves the steps necessary to restore data communications and computer capacity. This section contains actions assigned to specific individuals as well as special teams that may perform individually or collectively, at the discretion of the information systems manager.

Responsibility	Action
1. Information systems manager	Coordinate facilities restoration activities.
2. Building services	Coordinate reconstruction and equipment installation.
3. Operations manager	Restore operating system software, and data communications. Refer to Appendix for system recovery instructions. Coordinate local area network restoration activities with wide area network requirements.
4. Operations manager	Restore data bases and application software.
5. Operations manager	Ensure that remote data bases are synchronized with world headquarters.
6. Building manager	Provide engineering coordination, schedule construction and contract support, and expedite critical materials and installation schedules.

APPENDIX B

<u>EMERGENCY RESPONSE NOTIFICATION LIST</u>

<u>   Name   </u>   <u>   Street Address   </u>   <u>   Phone   </u>

See Normal Operations #24 and Emergency Response #16.

APPENDIX B

<u>EMPLOYEES WITH CELLULAR PHONES</u>

<u>   Name   </u>   <u>   Street Address   </u>   <u>   Phone   </u>

See Normal Operations #22 and Emergency Response #15.

APPENDIX B

MINIMUM OFFICE REQUIREMENTS

Department	Personnel	Phones	PCs/Modems
Flour Marketing	15	15	10
Special Commodities	40	40	20
Custom Farm Products	4	2	1
Customer Services	8	8	8
HQ Accounting	9	4	4
Flour Mill Marketing	3	3	3
Transporation	6	3	1
Grain Exchange Office	2	2	2
Totals	87	77	49

See Normal Operations #23 and Emergency Response #17.

APPENDIX B

RESTORATION PRIORITY LIST

1   TRADER WORKSTATION

2   CUSTOM FARM PRODUCTS POINT OF SALE

3   SCD INVOICING

4   FLOUR CONTRACTS

5   GRAIN CONTRACTS

6   FLOUR INVENTORY

7   FLOUR ORDER PROCESSING

8   FLOUR PRODUCTION AND SHIPMENTS

9   FLOUR PRICING

10 FLOUR INVOICING

11 BAKERY MIX

12 TRANSPORTATION RATES & ROUTES

13 ACCOUNTS RECEIVABLE

14 ACCOUNTS PAYABLE

15 GENERAL LEDGER

16 ELECTRONIC DATA INTERCHANGE

17 CAR TRACING

18 OFFICE AUTOMATION

19 MASTER PRODUCTION SCHEDULE

20 MAINTENANCE

21 DELIVERY/SALES ANALYSIS

22 FLOUR PRODUCT SPECIFICATIONS

23 FREIGHT BILL AUDIT

See Normal Operations #25 and Emergency Response #14.

APPENDIX C

SAMPLE BUSINESS CONTINUITY STRATEGIES

OVERVIEW

Business continuity strategies are established to document various options that are available to sustain vital business functions during a stabilization period. The specific options that are selected will depend on (1) the specific nature of the disaster, (2) the time that the disaster occurs, (3) the extent of damage, and (4) the prognosis for resuming operations in the same facility.

Management strategies have been formulated for the loss of digital voice and fax lines; loss of the mainframe; and temporary loss of access to buildings. These guidelines represent those options that are most likely to be used to ensure business continuity.

LOSS OF DIGITAL VOICE AND FAX LINES

Strategy

Rely on local telephone companies and long distance carrier to restore service. Immediately contact the long distance carrier to exploit whatever messaging options and rerouting capabilities are available to remote centers. Consider activation of the alternative facility.

Guidelines

Long Distance
- Use six backup analog phones.
- Use existing cellular phones or purchase new units.

Local
- Use cellular phones.
- Visit in person.
- Insert carrier disaster phone message.
- Activate alternative facility and adjust satellite call centers to address contingency plan priorities.
- Rent office space and expedite computer connectivity at another exchange.

- Reroute calls to external service bureau.
- Insert phone message after four rings, asking customers to fax or mail catalog order form.
- Reroute calls from space advertisements, direct sell advertisements, catalog requests, and "other questions" to external service bureau or have carrier block these specific type (separate telephone exchange) calls.
- Instruct carrier to capture phone numbers of uncompleted calls for special follow-up later.
- Consider shipping without credit approval.

LOSS OF MAINFRAME

Strategy

Marshall all available resources and authorize whatever expenses are necessary to eliminate waiting for paperwork to speed up the location, shipment, and installation of replacement hardware. Consider actions, such as chartering a plane, to improve delivery times. Schedule vendor and personnel to work around the clock. Assign full-time proactive expediters and coordinators to continually search for quicker ways to restore computer processing.

Advertising
- No impact

Circulation
- Based on the size and audience of a planned mailing, provide the mailer with a backup tape of a previous mailing (obtain from the mailer or use the MS backup copy) of either a premail type, ⅔ sample type, or large sample type; or have the mailer perform segmentation.
- Request MIS to print the latest copy of the customer average report from the backup tape.

Finance
- Defer accounts payable. Pay selected invoices manually.
- Use estimates for general ledger.

Merchandising, Buying, and Inventory Management
- Forecast manually.
- Use latest hard copy "demand analysis report" to order piece goods.
- Place purchase orders and expedite manually.
- Relocate skeleton workforce.
- Rent temporary office space.
- MIS install data lines to temporary office space.

Telemarketing and Customer Service
- Handwrite orders.
- Reroute overload calls to external service bureau.
- Inject carrier disaster message after four rings, asking customers to mail or fax order using catalog order form.
- Reroute calls from space advertisements, direct-sell advertisements, catalog requests, and "other questions" to external service bureau or have carrier block these exchange calls.
- Instruct carrier to capture phone number of uncompleted calls for special followup later.

Data Entry/Inmail/Banking Distribution Center
- Selectively process receipts and returns, or stage for processing after computer operations are restored.
- Use hard copy of active stock and stacker warehouse inventory locations to pick orders by hand.
- Add additional picking crews.
- Extend working hours.
- Pick from both active stock and warehouse stock.
- Rent additional scales and meters for shipping.
- Handwrite bills of lading and packing slips.

- Defer billing until computer processing is restored.
- Segregate in-process items for reconciliation later.

LOSS OF ACCESS TO BUILDING

Strategy

Temporarily stabilize operations in leased space while a determination is made as to where and when normal operations will be restored.

Advertising
- Retrieve off-site backups.
- Reshoot film.
- Rent temporary office space.

Buyers and Merchants
- Rent temporary office space.

Circulation
- Relocate.

Finance
- Relocate.

Telemarketing and Customer Service
- Adjust scripting to address expected delivery delays.
- Insert carrier disaster phone message.
- Rent office space and expedite computer connectivity at another exchange.
- Reroute calls to external service bureau.
- Insert phone message after four rings asking customers to fax or mail catalog order form.
- Reroute calls from space advertisements, direct-sell advertisements, catalog requests, and "other questions" to external service

bureau or have carrier block these specific-type (separate tele-phone exchange) calls.

- Have carrier capture phone numbers of uncompleted calls for special follow-up later.
- Consider shipping without credit approval.
- Revise floor credit limit authorization.

Data Entry/Inmail/Banking Distribution Center
- Notify customers with unshipped orders of delays.
- Notify vendors to hold shipments until further notice.
- Investigate other options for order fulfillment, such as selectively processing returns and receipts.

INSURANCE

Annuities

- Administration:
  Defer until computer processing capability is restored.
  Calculate fees manually.
- Premiums:
  Deposit cash.
  Defer cash application until computer processing capability is restored.
- Sales:
  Conduct business from residence.

Financial

- Administration:
  Defer until computer processing capability is restored.
- New deal sales:
  Model on local area network.

Defer updating until computer processing capability is restored.

Defer agreement creation and maintenance until computer processing capability is restored.

- Claims:

  Adjudicate manually.

  Defer postaudits until computer processing capability is restored.

- New sales:

  Manually prepare proposals containing provisions and lay terms.

  Prepare binder letters.

  Defer agreements until computer processing capability is restored.

- Renewals:

  Confirm block experience and characteristics by phone.

  Prepare proposals manually.

  Prepare letters of agreement manually.

  Defer amendments until computer processing capability is restored.

- Premiums:

  Deposit cash.

  Defer cash application until computer processing capability is restored.

HMO & Providers

- Claims:

  Adjudicate manually.

  Conduct postaudits.

- Premiums:

  Deposit cash in bank.

  Defer cash application until computer processing capability is restored.

- Rating:

    Defer rating until personal computer processing capability is restored.

- Health maintenance organization and provider:

    New Business:

    Obtain copies of similar client contracts.

    Renewals:

    Request copy of existing contract.

- Underwriting:

    New business—Request new underwriting information.

    Renewals—Request copy of existing contract.

Group General

Conduct business from residence.

- Administration:

    Conduct business from residences.

- Premiums:

    Continue operations at alternate locations.

- Claims:

    Recreate life claims from clients.

    Defer medical claims until computer processing capability is restored.

Self-Funded Markets

- Administration:

    Continue operations at alternate site.

- Claims:

    Request locations to courier claim reimbursement checks.

    Prepare checks manually.

- MedRe:

  Outside TPA continue operations.

  Defer annual accounting until computer processing capability is restored.

- Underwriting:

  Relocate personnel.

Domestic Individual Life & Health

- Claims:

  Recreate paper documents/adjudicate selective claims manually.

  Defer other claims until local area network computer processing capability is restored.

- Pricing/product development:

  Defer until computer processing capability is restored.

- Retrocession:

  New cases:

  Contact retrocessionaires to confirm capacity commitments.

  Audit client records.

  Renewals:

  Request copies of existing agreements.

- Sales:

  Conduct business from residence.

- Underwriting:

  Permit higher-caliber customers to exceed normal agreement limits.

  Use verbal approvals.

  Request duplicate papers for other pendings.

  Use express mail to transmit offers.

  Refer to retrocession records and client records to determine in-force and exposure on individuals.

International

- Claims:

  Adjudicate manually.

- Premiums:

  Deposit cash.

  Defer cash application until computer processing capability is restored.

- Sales:

  Defer until computer processing capability is restored.

  Prepare group quotes manually.

  Defer individual life quotes until computer processing capability is restored.

- Underwriting:

  New business—Request new underwriting information.

  Renewals—Request copy of existing agreement.

- Projects:

  Defer until computer processing capability is restored.

Long-Term Care

- Administration:

  Defer booking until computer processing capability is restored.

- Sales:

  Use personal computer for quoting or defer until computer processing capability is restored.

PAX

- Claims:

  Adjudicate manually.

- New deal pricing:

  Defer until computer processing capability is restored.

- Pool accounting:

    Defer until computer processing capability is restored.

- Premiums:

    Deposit cash.

    Defer cash application until computer processing capability is restored.

- Renewals:

    Request provisional extensions.

SUPPORT SERVICES

Actuarial

Defer until computer processing capability is restored.

Agreements and Regulatory Compliance

Request reporting extensions.

Financial Services

- Disbursements:

    Use corporate system to pay invoices previously vouchered.

    Selectively pay other invoices manually.

- Financial Statements:

    Request filing extensions.

    Use estimates or "plan."

- Planning:

    Defer until computer processing capability is restored.

    Receipts:

    Deposit cash.

    Defer cash application until computer processing capability is restored.

Defer delinquency calls until computer processing capability is restored.

Medical

- Research and development:
  Defer until computer processing capability is restored.
- Underwriting consulting:
  Travel to underwriter location.

Strategic Planning

Defer until computer processing capability is restored.

Support

- Communications:
  Defer standard publications until computer processing capability is restored.
- Human resources:
  Defer until computer processing capability is restored.
- Payroll:
  Duplicate latest payroll.
  Prepare manual checks as needed.
- Training:
  Defer until computer processing capability is restored.

GLOSSARY

Business as usual Operating under normal conditions, that is, without any significant interruption of operations as a result of a disaster.

Business continuity strategies Guidelines that outline how specific activities will be performed until normal processing capability is restored and buildings are accessible.

Business function The most elementary activities, for example, calculating gross pay, updating job descriptions, matching invoices to receiving reports.

Business impact analysis A study to estimate the effect that a specific disaster/incident might have on a given operation or activity.

Cold site A backup computer site without computer hardware. All environmental components, such as power, air conditioning, and data communications are installed. Theoretically, a computer cold site could be operational within a few hours or days following delivery of hardware.

Declaration fee A one-time charge paid to a computer backup hot-site (or cold-site) provider at the time a disaster is officially declared.

Disaster An incident of such severity and magnitude that emergency steps are needed to stay in business.

Disaster recovery life cycle Consists of (1) normal operations—the period of time before a disaster occurs, (2) emergency response—the hours or days immediately following a disaster, (3) interim processing—the period of time from the occurrence of a disaster until temporary operations are restored, and (4) restoration—returning to normal.

Emergency response period See disaster recovery life cycle.

First-line supervisor The level of management just above hourly employees or clerical staff.

Hot site A backup computer site with compatible hardware installed.

Localized disaster   An incident that affects only a single building or area.

Mobile site   Either a hot site or cold site on wheels; usually one or more large trailers.

Normal operations   See disaster recovery life cycle.

Notification list   A list of key individuals to be contacted, usually in the event of a disaster. Notification lists normally contain phone numbers and addresses, which may be used in the event that telephones are not operational.

Off-site location   A location usually at least several hundred yards or more from a facility that could incur a disaster.

Positioning   The process of making others feel comfortable with your strategy, style, and methodology of contingency plan development.

Reciprocal agreement   When two different organizations mutually agree to back up each other's processing capability in the event that either one incurs a disaster.

Redundant backup site   Any of two or more data centers that could (by temporarily decreasing their own workload) assume the processing load of critical applications from another data center.

Service bureau   A data processing utility that provides processing capability, normally for specialized processing, such as payroll.

Shell facility   See cold site.

Stabilization period   The period of time between the occurrence of a disaster and the time when normal operations are restored.

Subscription fee   Normally, monthly fees paid for the privilege of using (for purposes described in this book) a backup computer hot site or cold site, on a first-come, first-served basis.

Vital business functions   Those specific business activities that have a significant impact on cash flow or servicing customer orders.

Window   The length of time it is expected to take (under emergency conditions, with adequate resources) to restore whatever processing capability was destroyed in a disaster.

INDEX

INDEX